MW00965715

10~

Jacki Passmore

fast & fiery

a cookbook about chilli & other hot things

First published in 1999 by
Anne O'Donovan Pty Ltd
171 La Trobe Street,
Melbourne 3000

Copyright © Jacki Passmore 1999

This book is copyright. Apart from fair dealing for the purpose of private study, research, criticism or review, as permitted under the Copyright Act, no part may be reproduced by any process without the written permission of the publisher.

Designed by Danie Pout
Edited by Sarah Dawson
Photography by Simon Griffiths
Food styling by Deborah McLean
Author photo by Mark Burgin

Typeset by J & M Typesetting
Printed in Australia by Australian Print Group, Maryborough, Victoria
Distributed by Penguin Books Australia Ltd

National Library of Australia
Cataloguing-in-publication entry
    Passmore, Jacki.
    Fast and fiery.

    Includes index.
    ISBN 1 876 026 27 8

    1. Cookery (Spices). 2. Cookery (Hot peppers). I. Title.

    641.6384

Contents

Introduction

'Never cook in haste or anger!' Words of advice from a talented amateur cook to a young food writer. She had much to teach me about the enjoyment and practicalities of cooking. This improbable guru of my early food career could whip up a guaranteed no-flop soufflé while checking her ten-year-old's homework and discussing the new colour scheme for her house refurbishment with her decorator. 'When I am not happy to cook, we go out or order in. When I am short on time, I cheat!' She would glide around her well-organised kitchen with the fluid movements of a dancer. Cooking for her was theatre, recreation and meditation, not just meeting the needs of her family. Her time in the kitchen was to be enjoyed. Day to day, she performed culinary magic on simple, fresh ingredients. When time and inspiration allowed, she braved adventurous projects like towering croquembouche and whole pigs roasted on smouldering coconut husks and hot rocks in an earth oven. This ultimate hostess cooked cleverly, with natural ease and flair, never compromising on quality and flavour. Our paths diverged, but I remained a disciple of her tenets.

Today's food is very much about cooking with ease, yet achieving full, bold flavours. It is about having the confidence to cut corners without jeopardising the end result. It is about being courageous with seasonings and ingredients, and inventive with cooking styles. It is a brave, cross-cultural interchange.

That is what *Fast and Fiery* is about. Here are dishes designed for ease and speed, meals to be prepared in under half an hour. Here is a pungent collection of recipes from chilli-eating countries and other food cultures fired up not only with chilli in its many guises, but with Japanese wasabi, Indian mustard, North African harissa, and the Sichuan spice which we know as Chinese pepper but the Japanese call sansho. The flavours vary from fragrantly fierce to seductively piquant. You can turn on as much heat as you like. If caution is called for, plan a meal around one red-hot dish. But for unrestrained chilli addicts, the dishes can be mixed and matched in scintillating menus that take the fiery experience right through to the pud.

Hot Chilli Gossip

A long and fruitful journey

Mexico is the native habitat of the chilli plant, and its presence there can be dated back to 6000 BC. So, with salt, this ferociously flavoured fruit is one of our earliest food seasonings. In those ancient times, chillies were known only in Central and South America. The western world had to wait until the end of the fifteenth century for the arrival of this messiah of the kitchen, delivered courtesy of the Spanish and Portuguese colonisers of the New World.

Garcia Orta, a Portuguese chronicler, wrote in 1593, 'This capsicum or Indian pepper is diligently cultivated in castles by gardeners and also by women in their kitchens and house gardens'. In truth, chillies were mostly grown on hallowed ground by monks, and most domestic Iberian cooks preferred the other new foods from the cargoholds of the galleons: tomatoes, eggplants, potatoes and the sweeter capsicum. The imperial kitchens introduced chillies to court menus, but the royals were more enthused by grander imports from their new protectorates – the gold of the Incas and the emeralds of Peru.

But the traders' tastebuds had been seduced by chillies on the other side of the world. So, undeterred by the lukewarm welcome for chillies at home, they loaded their hot and spicy cargo back onto giant oceangoing vessels and continued on to more receptive markets in Africa, India and Southeast Asia. By the end of the sixteenth century, chillies had become an indispensable seasoning for hundreds of millions of people, trading posts were flourishing and home crops had taken root. Chillies were festooned in scarlet banners over doorways and ceiling beams in

Kashmir and Afghanistan. They became intrinsic to African cuisines from Ethiopia to Algeria. In Burma and Thailand, they dethroned locally grown pepper as a seasoning. They brought winter warmth to snow-bound Tibetans and wind-chilled Mongolians. And meanwhile back in the Americas, they infiltrated the cuisines of the southern states and the nearby island countries of the Caribbean.

That fresh chillies turned out to be rich in vitamin C, and dried chillies high in vitamin A, was a bonus not lost on Chinese herbalists. They prescribed chillies for all manner of ailments, citing them as particularly useful for the treatment of colds and flu-related viral conditions. When the charismatic young revolutionary, Mao Tse Tung, assembled his disciples in 1935 for their long march from central China to overthow the seats of power in the north, he packed chillies, garlic and ginger for the journey. This triumvirate of flavour-potent natural medicaments sustained the straggly groups of radicals in body and spirit throughout their arduous journey into the history books.

Chilli varieties

Chillies are easily grown in warm gardens or indoor pots, and usually produce prolifically.

As a rule, the smaller the chilli the hotter it will be. Red chillies are simply ripe green chillies and are not necessarily hotter: the world's hottest chilli, the habanero, is an innocuous pale orange colour. Chilli heat may vary from fruit to fruit, depending on the climate, soil and other growing considerations.

Your choice of a particular chilli for a dish will depend on several factors – colour, heat, sweetness, depth of flavour, and size. Drying chillies intensifies their flavour but not their heat, making them the choice of many Asian cooks when preparing curry pastes. Roasting and smoking further enhances flavour and colour, and tends to minimise heat. Following is a short list of the popular varieties and their characteristics (average length is given in brackets).

ANCHO   A large, triangular, mahogany-coloured dried chilli sold only in specialty shops: mild to medium heat. Use for sauces and Mexican moles.

BANANA   (sometimes called Hungarian wax chilli) A long, wide-shouldered, pale-green chilli: mild heat. Use for stuffings, salads and pickled dishes.

BIRD'S EYE   (Thai: *prik khee noo suan*) The smallest chilli (2 cm or 1 in.), multi-coloured: very hot.

CAYENNE AND TABASCO   Small, bullet-shaped red or orange chilli (5 cm or 2 in.) which is made into cayenne pepper and tabasco sauce: more heat than flavour. Use fresh.

CHERRY PEPPER (sometimes called Hungarian)   Ball-shaped, thick-fleshed red chilli (4 cm or 1¾ in.): mild to hot.

DUTCH RED   Long, curved, tapering chilli (11 cm or 4½ in.) with thick flesh and sweet, fresh flavour: medium-hot. Use for chilli pastes and sauces, and general cooking. Can be roasted or pickled.

FIESTA   Short, tapered, multi-coloured ornamental. Use as a garnish.

HABANERO (Scotch bonnet is closely related)   Irregular, box- or bell-shaped chilli, green to golden-orange when ripe. The hottest chilli.

JALAPENO   Short, wide shouldered, smooth-skinned red and green chilli (5 cm or 2 in.): medium-hot. Use fresh, or pickled in vinegar or brine.

KOREAN, STANDARD   Medium-length green chilli (5 cm or 2 in.) with thin flesh and a hot vegetable flavour. Use fresh, or pickled in vinegar.

PIMIENTO/PAPRIKA   Fleshy, heart-shaped sweet pepper.

SERRANO   Smooth-skinned, short, scarlet and green chilli (3 cm or 1½ in.): hot (use 3 small Thai chillies to 1 serrano).

THAI, SMALL (*prik khee noo*)   Short, very slender, pointed red or deep-green chilli (5 cm or 2 in.) with thin flesh and lots of seeds: very hot. Use fresh or dried in chilli pastes and curry pastes.

THAI, STANDARD (*prik chee faa*)   Medium-sized green and red chilli (8 cm or 3 in.): medium to hot. For general use.

Handling and preparing chillies

The heat of chillies comes from *capsaicin*, a bitter alkaloid concentrated mostly in the seeds and internal fibres, ribs and veins. *Capsaicin* is an irritant on direct contact, and is not destroyed by heating or freezing. So handle chillies with care:

• Wear rubber or disposable latex gloves.

• Try to hold chillies by the stem, or make contact with the skin side not the inside surface.

• Wash all surfaces, including your knife, with soapy water after handling.

• Avoid touching eyes or skin after handling.

• Keep face away while roasting, frying or dry-frying chillies: the fumes are potent and will irritate throat, nose, eyes and facial skin.

Managing the heat

• Roll chillies across a work surface, pressing firmly: this loosens the seeds and fibres and releases some of the hot enzymes into them, so the chillies are less hot once they have been de-seeded.

• To make hot chillies milder, soak in 3 parts vinegar to 1 part salt for 1 hour. Rinse before use.

• To decrease heat in a highly chillied or spiced dish, add sugar, cream, yoghurt or starchy vegetables like potatoes.

• To soothe a chilli-burned mouth, suck an ice-cube or drink dairy products, strong alcohol or sweet drinks. Cold beer and water briefly numb the burning, but may increase the irritation.

Bringing out flavour

• Soak dried chillies in boiling water before grinding for use in chilli pastes and curry pastes.

• Home-made chilli pastes have a fresher flavour than commercial ones, which contain vinegar.

- Roasting chillies in a dry pan over medium heat introduces rich, smoky flavours. Place under a hot grill or in a non-stick or iron pan, and cook slowly for about 2 minutes on each side. The smokier the better, if it is flavour you want, but take care not to burn them.

Shredding, slicing and chopping

- To slice whole chillies, hold the stem and begin at the point, cutting diagonally.
- To de-seed, slit along the length from shoulder to point and use the tip of a small knife to scrape out the seeds and fibres.
- To shred, place de-seeded chilli flat on a board, skin down. Use a small sharp knife to cut across in fine shreds, or lengthwise into long strips (they will curl if placed in iced water).
- To chop, place de-seeded or whole chillies on a board. Use a Chinese cleaver or large heavy cook's knife, chopping coarsely at first and then continuing until the chillies are finely minced.

Hot tips from around the world

Japan

- Sprinkle shichimi togarashi (a seven-spice mix based on chilli) over noodles, soups and vegetables.
- Add wasabi powder and salt to flour for coating fried fish, or beat wasabi paste into tempura or other batter.

China

- Investigate uses for that potent seasoning, Sichuan or Chinese pepper. Sprinkle over stir-fries, eggs, noodles and vegetables and, with moderation, into soups. It can be numbingly hot.
- Make a sauce of soy sauce and sliced green chillies to serve with boiled seafood or fried chicken.

India

- Add garam masala or crushed cumin seeds and a pinch of chilli powder to batter for frying fish.
- Brush tandoori or vindaloo paste over steaks, sausages or chops before grilling.
- Serve hot mango or other chutney with Aussie standards like meat pies, barbecued sausages or a steak.

The Pacific

- Try sweet chilli sauce over scrambled or fried eggs.
- Include halved fresh chillies, small raw eggplants and raw green beans in the vegetable selection you serve with dips.

Europe

- Put a shaker of chilli flakes on the table when you serve pasta.
- Drop a small hot red chilli into your jar of salad vinaigrette.
- For a kick-start to the day, spread buttered toast with harissa or chilli sauce before topping with baked beans.

The Americas

- Look for chimmichurri green sauce in stores where Mexican foods are sold. It's a zinger.
- Lightly shake tabasco over natural oysters, and flood with lime juice.
- Toss chopped pickled chillies through salads, or add them to hamburgers.
- Sprinkle a few drops of tabasco into an ice-cold beer for refreshment with a big kick – real southern comfort.
- Sprinkle tabasco and icing sugar over sliced strawberries.

The Caribbean

- Steep hot chillies in sherry and use in stir-fries and sautées.

International

- Shake chilli-flavoured oils into stir-fries, sauces and salad dressings, and over seafood or grills.
- Always travel with your favourite chilli sauce.
- Add a sprinkle of chilli powder or flakes to the cheese topping for a mornay dish.
- Steep a hot chilli in gin or vodka for peppy cocktails.
- Add a pinch of black pepper to freshly brewed coffee.
- Add chilli flakes and black pepper to dry breadcrumbs.
- Stir chilli sauce into clear honey as a zingy dip for fried snacks.
- Season salt for fries with chilli powder (or cayenne) and garlic salt.

Some chilli trivia

- One of the hottest Mexican salsas is as sharp as its bite. *Pico de gallo salsa*, which translates as 'rooster's beak', includes small hot radishes, or Japanese horseradish, and at least three kinds of chillies.
- With a chilli heat rating of 200,000–350,000 Scoville units, the *habanero* is the world's hottest chilli.
- Eating a single hot chilli can raise the metabolism enough to burn 45 calories of a 700-calorie meal.
- *Ristras* are the clustered strings of red chillies the Mexicans tie and hang for drying at harvest time.
- Uncovered on the Net, this comment from a cowboy, Bones Hooks, a chilli lover: 'Lord God, chilli eaters is some of Your chosen people. We don't know why You're so doggone good to us. But never think we ain't grateful … Amen.'
- Wasabi, Japanese horseradish, has a heat rating to rival the hottest chilli. Indispensable to sushi and sashimi, it is also a short-term treatment for sinus congestion.

- The Spanish christened the chilli *pimiento* (grammatically masculine), it being viewed as stronger and better than *pimienta* (pepper).
- Chillies help increase gastrointestinal secretions, and are now being used in treatment of duodenal ulcers, whereas once they were believed to have been one of the causes.
- In the West Indies, one variety of chilli is known as *bouda a Man Jacques*, 'Madame Jacques's bum', for its rounded form.
- Sichuan pepper is not related to common black pepper, but is the fruit buds of the prickly ash tree native to north China and Japan (where the spice is called *sansho*).
- Cayenne pepper capsules can improve blood circulation and warm chilly toes.
- In many parts of the world, chillies are believed to ward off the evil eye. Dried chillies are hung in the eaves or burned in the kitchen to intimidate bad spirits.
- Mustard got its name from grape must (unfermented grape juice), which in the Middle Ages was mixed with the crushed seeds to make the hot condiment.
- Green, white and black pepper come from the same plant. Green is the fresh buds, black the dried buds, and white the polished black buds.
- The chilli sniffle is a reflex response to chillies, producing nasal drip. Gustatory rhinitis is not an allergy but a reaction to the stimulation of chemical receptors in the mouth.

The Entertainers

THIS CHAPTER IS a kaleidoscope of easy party food, which would also fit the bill as no-fuss TV and fireside snacks for a quiet night with friends. Many of the dishes would also make a deliciously spicy prelude to a sit-down dinner.

Guests always appreciate home-made munchies at a party. Finger food makes for simple and practical entertaining, and minimises clean-ups after the event. Allow five or six portions for each guest at a party of shortish duration, and at least half that much again if it looks like the night may swing on. An ample supply of fresh bread with chunks of cheese or cold meat would provide extra ballast for the ravenous.

If you are taking the time and trouble to cook, there is nothing wrong with blatantly seeking compliments for your effort. Dazzle your friends with a collage of savoury bites like the Thai fish cakes, chorizo empanadas and chicken sticks with coriander chilli mayo, piled onto one huge platter and gregariously garnished with sprays of fresh chillies. And to accompany the dips, make an extravagant presentation of fresh vegetables and piled fingers of crusty breads: perhaps offer two or three dips, not just a single lonely bowl. Fill colourful dishes with crunchy nibbles, to eat by the handful.

Finally, don't leave yourself out of the party. Balance the workload by serving a mix of hot dishes which require last-minute attention, and cold foods you have prepared in advance.

Fast and fiery entertaining

Feel no guilt about using deli purchases, pre-made pastries and breads, and ready-to-cook products for fast and flashy entertaining. Dress them to impress. Invent exciting cross-cultural combinations. Present them with pizzazz and serve with confidence.

- Arrange slices of *roast pork or turkey* on a platter with small dishes of the following, for dipping: minced garlic in fish sauce, sweet chilli sauce, and spicy peanut sauce (page 104) .
- Roll *cold cuts* around strips of roasted capsicum or eggplant, with a smear of chilli sauce and a basil leaf or sprig of coriander. Pierce with toothpicks.
- Grill or fry *pork or seafood balls* purchased from Asian stores, and serve with a hot or sweet chilli dip.
- Cut the breast of a purchased *Chinese roast duck* into thin slices, and dice the remaining meat. Combine diced meat with roasted hazelnuts, diced celery, diced green apple, water chestnuts or nashi, and chopped shallots. Toss with mayonnaise spiked with hot chilli sauce or wasabi. Mound in the centre of plates on a few rocket or small lettuce leaves and drape the sliced breast meat over. *Or* roll strips of Chinese duck in bought duck pancakes, with cucumber sticks and hoisin sauce spiked with sambal ulek or hot chilli sauce. Or, in Chinese soup spoons, serve diced Chinese duck with a dollop of hot red curry sauce and a drizzle of coconut cream.
- For *chicken Caesar*, fry small pieces of crumbed chicken in olive oil with diced bacon and cubed bread. Beat an egg into a half cup of mayonnaise, fold through the fried ingredients and spread over a cos-leaf salad.
- For *Mexican chicken*, place crumbed chicken fillets on an oven tray and cook at 180°C (375°F) for about 25 minutes, basting with a little olive oil. Cover with Mexican salsa and generous grated cheese, and return to the oven until the cheese bubbles.
- De-bone and dice a *smoked chicken*, place in a bowl and add enough sour cream and hot mango chutney to bind and moisten. Cut squares of thawed puff pastry, fill with the chicken mixture and fold into envelope shapes. Bake in a hot oven for about 15 minutes. (Alternatively, wrap in 4 layers of buttered filo pastry.)
- A quick and easily assembled entrée: make a *vegetarian stack* with layers of oil-marinated roasted capsicum and eggplant, large basil leaves, slices of goat cheese or marinated feta, and a hot salsa into which you have mixed capers and diced semi-dried tomatoes. Surround with a salad of small leaves dressed with olive oil and balsamic vinegar.

- For a *Japanese-style smoked salmon stack*, spread one side of bought crepes with spreadable cream cheese into which you have beaten wasabi and soy sauce. Cover with smoked salmon and chopped nori seaweed. Stack the crepes, the top one spread with wasabi cream and sprinkled with chopped nori and toasted sesame seeds. Cut into wedges to serve. Or use bought mini pancakes and finish each small stack with $\frac{1}{2}$ teaspoon of wasabi-flavoured flying fish roe.
- Fry purchased *mini dim sims* and serve with hot barbecue or chilli sauce.
- Oven-heat *samosas or curry puffs* and serve with a bought tamarind sauce.
- Make tasty crostini by spreading toasted baguette with mashed *sardines in hot sauce*.
- Stack crackers with peppered pastrami or hot salami and smoky cheese, and top with a pickled chilli or cocktail onion.
- Serve cucumber sticks with a dip of bought tsatsiki or hommus onto which you have swirled a little chilli oil.
- Grill African *merguez sausages*, and serve with a sweet-hot chutney or chilli jam.
- Slit open purchased *Indian flat breads* or thin pita bread, and fill with cooked potato or lentils mashed with chopped spring onions, chopped green chillis, salt, and garam masala. Warm in a hot oven and brush with butter before serving as a light vegetarian snack with a sweet chutney.

Chilli-lovers' antipasto platter

A selection of nibbles is an easy way to entertain ravenous chilli-lovers. Serve with sliced baguette or a chewy Italian bread such as ciabatta. Alternatively, toast the bread lightly or grill it on a ribbed hotplate, then spread with mashed anchovies, olive tapenade or pesto. Choose colourful garnishes: frilled-edge lettuces of several colours, radishes, cherry tomatoes, a sprig of chillies from your garden, olives or caperberries from a jar.

You might like to add the crunchy element of crisp-fried whitebait or garlic croutons, or grilled baby octopus seasoned with a slick of olive oil, a squeeze of lemon and scattering of garlic and coarsely cracked pepper.

Arrange the components on individual plates or assemble on one huge platter for guests to help themselves. Choose from the following ideas, allowing about 6 pieces per person as an entrée, and at least 8 for a main course.

- *canned sardines* If in hot tomato sauce, use as they are. If packed in oil, drain and dress with finely chopped onion and/or chillies, or tomato sauce spiked with chilli.
- *peppered smoked mackerel* Skin and break into chunks.
- *hard-boiled eggs* Halve lengthwise and mash yolks with chilli sauce and minced celery or chopped coriander.
- *marinated olives* (drained).
- *giardiniera* or other pickled vegetables, including chillies (drained).
- *artichokes in oil* Season with garlic, pepper and chilli.
- *chorizo* Cut into thick chunks.
- *marinated mussels* Sprinkle with chilli oil.
- *feta or parmesan* chunks Skewer with stuffed green olives.
- *cherry tomatoes* (whole or halved).
- *paper-thin slices of prosciutto* Wrap around pickled chillies.
- *grilled red capsicum or eggplant* marinated in oil.
- *bocconcini cheeses* Halve them and marinate in oil with herbs and chilli.
- *pepper pecorino or cumin-flavoured havarti* Cut into chunks.
- *a selection of deli meats* Use peppery salami, pancetta or pastrami.
- *marinated button mushrooms* (page 10)

Chilli cheese dip

Dips go a long way when served with vegetables, cracker biscuits, or pita bread wedges.

250 g (8 oz) spreadable cream cheese
150 ml (5 fl. oz) sour cream
½ teaspoon salt
2–3 teaspoons hot chilli sauce (Thai sriracha is excellent)
1 teaspoon sweet paprika
1 teaspoon crushed pink peppercorns
2 teaspoons dill tips or 1 tablespoon finely chopped basil or parsley

Place everything except the peppercorns and herbs in a food processor. Whiz to a thick cream, then swirl in the peppercorns and herbs. Transfer the dip to a serving bowl.

Witloof leaves, celery or cucumber sticks, slices of green capsicum, small white button mushrooms and carrot sticks are excellent with this creamy dip.

Serves 12–15

Holy guacamole

Serve with tortilla chips or warmed pita points. Or push the pain threshold with toast fingers spread while hot with a chilli- or peppercorn-flavoured butter.

1 large ripe avocado
1 spring onion, very finely chopped
1 tablespoon mayonnaise
2–3 teaspoons sweet chilli sauce
a shake (or three) of tabasco
1 teaspoon chopped coriander or basil
salt and pepper

Mash everything together with a fork, leaving it slightly textural.

Serves 4–6

 Tortilla chips go well with Mexican-style dips. To make them, cut wheat tortillas into strips 12 mm (½ in.) wide. Heat oil in a wok or deep-fryer and fry the chips until crisp. Remove with a slotted spoon, drain well and pile onto a platter over a paper towel.

Hot and creamy corn dip

A chunky dip which goes well with celery or carrot sticks, tortilla chips or taco crisps.

1 cup corn kernels (fresh, frozen or canned)
1 red chilli, de-seeded and chopped
1 green chilli, de-seeded and chopped
1 spring onion, chopped
2 tablespoons olive oil or butter
1 teaspoon ground cumin
1½ tablespoons plain flour
1½ cups sour cream
½ cup grated vintage cheddar
bacon chips and/or chopped coriander (optional)
salt

Drain or thaw corn kernels, as required. Boil in lightly salted water for 4 minutes or microwave on High for 2 minutes. Drain well.

Sauté the chillies and spring onion in the olive oil or butter for about 1 minute. Add the cumin and flour, and stir for a few seconds before adding the sour cream. Stir until the sauce thickens, then stir in the corn, cheese, bacon chips and/or coriander, and salt to taste. Serve hot or at room temperature.

Serves 12

Green olive and chilli tapenade

This is a cinch to make, just the thing to serve with chunky Italian bread or warmed pita when friends drop in unexpectedly. It will keep for a few weeks in a covered jar in the fridge.

Toss a big handful of capsicum-stuffed olives into a food processor with a slurp of oil and whatever chilli product is closest to hand – sauce, purée, powder or oil. Using the pulse control, grind the olives until somewhere between chunky and smooth: you need a bit of texture. That's it, except perhaps for a garnish such as chopped chives or chilli.

Serves 6–8

 Marinated mushrooms are a delicious addition to an antipasto platter and will keep for a week or two in the refrigerator. Select small button mushrooms and rinse in cold water. Place in a non-aluminium saucepan with a mixture of water and white vinegar to barely cover: add a sprinkle of rosemary spikes, black peppercorns and a crumble of dried chilli, and balance the flavours with sugar and salt. Bring to the boil and simmer for 3–4 minutes, then cool.

Spicy bean dip with nachos

A flavour-packed dip to whip up in seconds. If you have some tomato chilli chutney (page 23) use $1/4$ cup of it with $1/4$ cup tomato-based pasta sauce instead of a purchased salsa.

The dip

a 375-g can kidney beans or bean mix, drained

$1/2$ cup Mexican salsa

1 tablespoon chopped coriander or basil (optional)

To assemble the nachos

1 large pack chilli corn chips

$1 1/2$ cups chopped roast chicken (optional)

$1 1/2$ cups grated cheddar or other tasty cheese

To serve

1 cup salsa

1 cup sour cream

1 cup mashed avocado, seasoned with salt, pepper and lemon juice

Preheat the oven to 220°C (425°F). Place all the dip ingredients in a food processor and grind to a smooth purée.

To assemble the nachos, spread a third of the corn chips in a large oven dish or microwave dish and cover with the bean dip and the chopped chicken. Top with the remaining corn chips and the cheese. Place in the preheated oven for about 8 minutes (or microwave on High for about 2 minutes), until the cheese melts. Serve with the salsa, sour cream and avocado.

Makes $1 1/2$ cups of dip

Crunchy peppered bay prawns

Very small bay prawns are usually inexpensive, as most people can't be bothered with the tedium of peeling them. When you find some at your market, buy a kilo and invite friends over. Fried to a crunch, then sprinkled with a spicy salt and served on paper with pre-dinner drinks, they beat beer nuts any day.

There is no need even to rinse the prawns, but place them in a colander for about an hour (or toss them in a kitchen cloth) so any surface moisture dries off. Heat deep oil: you will need at least 3 cups of a flavourless vegetable oil. When it's very, very hot, slide in about 2 cups of prawns and fry until they are so crisp they rustle in the pan. Remove with a wire scoop to a colander or tray lined with paper towels. Sprinkle a spicy salt (page 14) evenly over, stir them around a bit, and serve this batch while you prepare a second.

Leftovers, when completely cold, can be stored in an airtight container and given a very quick refry to crisp them up again. Any oil you have left can be kept in a marked container in the refrigerator, to use for cooking seafood.

Serves 8–10

Cajun popcorn

Fantastic entertainers, these crispy battered puffs are seasoned with cajun spices. Instead of the prawns, you can use diced vegetables (parcooked as needed), chicken, tofu, or even cheese, or you could take advantage of broken fresh prawn meat, which is usually good value. The pieces should be small enough to earn their name popcorn. Serve a mound with small forks or toothpicks, or tumble them into lettuce cups as an entrée with a dipping sauce of vinegar and chopped chilli. If you do not have cajun spices on hand, use Indian garam masala with a pinch of crushed thyme and chilli powder.

½ cup plain flour
500 g (1 lb) small peeled cooked prawns
3 egg whites
1 cup self-raising flour
1 teaspoon baking powder
2 teaspoons cajun seasoning
1 tablespoon chopped coriander leaves or parsley (optional)
1 teaspoon onion or garlic salt
⅔ cup water, buttermilk or milk
oil for deep-frying

Place the plain flour in a plastic bag, add the prawns and shake well to coat evenly. Pour into the dried colander and shake off any excess flour.

Make a batter with the egg whites, self-raising flour, baking powder, spices, herbs and salt, adding enough chilled water, buttermilk or milk to make it the consistency of thick cream.

Heat deep oil to very hot, and have ready a tray or rack lined with paper towels. Tip the prawns into the batter, and use a slotted spoon to transfer them in batches to the oil. It does not matter if a few stick together, but make sure they do not form large lumps. Fry until the batter is puffy and golden, then retrieve and drain. When they are all cooked, serve at once.

Serves 10 as party food, or 4–6 as an entrée

Devil's wings

Great party food for chilli fiends, these can be served with rice or salad as an entrée and go really well on a buffet table. Although they can be cooked in a microwave in only about 10 minutes, a conventional oven gives the most delectable result.

10 chicken wings (about 750 g or 1½ lb)
1 tablespoon hot chilli sauce
1 tablespoon hot mustard
2 tablespoons teriyaki marinade
¾ teaspoon salt
1 teaspoon black pepper
2 teaspoons sugar
1 tablespoon vegetable oil
2 tablespoons water

Preheat the oven to 200°C (400°F). Segment the chicken wings, giving 30 pieces in all. In a glass or ceramic oven dish, combine the remaining ingredients and then add the chicken pieces. Turn them over and over to coat evenly with the seasonings. Place in the centre of the preheated oven to cook for about 25 minutes, turning occasionally.

Makes 30 pieces

Chicken sticks with coriander chilli mayonnaise

Prepare the mayonnaise first, to allow the flavours to develop.

The mayo

¾ cup mayonnaise

1 green chilli, de-seeded and finely chopped

2 tablespoons finely chopped coriander leaves

⅓ teaspoon crushed garlic

½ teaspoon salt

The chicken sticks

400 g (13 oz) chicken tenderloins or breast fillets

1 cup cornflour

1 teaspoon cracked black pepper

1 teaspoon paprika

2 teaspoons garlic salt

2 tablespoons water

4 cups vegetable or light olive oil

Whisk the mayonnaise ingredients together in a small mixing bowl, then cover and set aside.

Cut chicken tenderloins into 3–4 diagonal slices, or cut breast meat into narrow strips about 5 cm (2 in.) long. In a mixing bowl combine the cornflour, pepper, paprika, garlic salt and water. Stir well: the batter should be smooth and thick. Heat oil in a wok or large pan over medium–high heat. Dip the chicken pieces one by one into the batter and place carefully in the oil. Fry for about a minute, until golden, pushing the chicken below the surface of the oil so it cooks evenly. For best results, cook in several batches. Remove with a slotted spoon and drain on absorbent paper for a few minutes.

Reheat the oil and quickly fry the chicken a second time, just to crisp. Lift out and drain. Serve hot, with the mayonnaise for dipping.

Serves 4–6

Jalapeno chicken fritters

You can make these tasty little fritters bite-sized to serve on toothpicks as party food, or larger to serve over shredded lettuce as a first course.

350 g (11 oz) minced chicken
2 jalapeno chillies, de-seeded and roughly chopped
1 large spring onion, roughly chopped
2 tablespoons roughly chopped coriander
1 slice of fresh white bread, crusts removed, torn
1 large egg
1 teaspoon self-raising flour (or mashed potato)
1 cup vegetable or light olive oil
sweet chilli sauce or Mexican salsa

Place the chicken, chillies, spring onion, coriander, bread, egg and salt in a food processor and grind to a paste. Add the flour or mashed potato, and mix well.

Heat the oil in a wok or large pan. Using a teaspoon, scoop little heaps of the mixture into the oil to fry until golden, turning and stirring them around to ensure they cook evenly (about 2 minutes). Alternatively, use a tablespoon to scoop larger portions into the oil, pressing them with a spatula or the back of a spoon to flatten them to about 12 mm (1 in.). Cook for 1½ minutes on each side, then remove with a slotted spoon. Drain for a few minutes on paper towels, then serve with sweet chilli sauce or Mexican salsa.

Serves 4

Peperoni pizza fingers

Great party fare and also delicious as a snack for all occasions.

a piece of focaccia 25 × 8 cm (10 × 3½ in.)
1–2 tablespoons olive oil (optional)
2 tablespoons pesto
15 thin slices peppered salami or peperoni, chopped
½ cup semi-dried tomatoes, chopped
1 small onion, very finely chopped
1½ tablespoons capers, finely chopped
2 tablespoons pitted black olives, chopped
¾ cup grated melting cheese (e.g. mozzarella or cheddar)

Preheat the oven to 220°C (425°F). Slit the focaccia in half horizontally and place the two pieces, cut side upwards, on a baking sheet. Combine the oil (if used) and pesto, and spread evenly over the bread, then top with the salami, tomatoes, onion, capers and olives. Spread the cheese evenly over, place the pizza in the oven and cook for about 12 minutes. Cut each piece in half if serving as a snack, or into fingers for party food, and serve at once.

Makes 20 pieces

Mediterranean roll-ups

Everyone loves this classic combination of Mediterranean flavours. Line up the rolls on a platter, or nestle them into a curly endive salad as an entrée. If you cannot source soft, semi-dried tomatoes of the right size, it's easy to make your own (see page 53).

24 semi-dried tomato halves
12 large, marinated black olives
1 large red chilli, de-seeded and chopped
12 anchovy fillets, halved
48 capers, drained
24 basil leaves
extra-virgin olive oil
black pepper
salt
toothpicks

Place the tomatoes, cut side upwards, on a worktop. With a small sharp knife pare the flesh from the olives and divide this between the tomatoes. Scatter the chopped chilli evenly over, then add 1 piece of anchovy, 2 capers and a basil leaf to each tomato. Add a few drops of olive oil to each, and season with salt and pepper. Roll up the tomatoes, starting with the stem end, and secure with toothpicks. They can be served at once, but if time allows chill them for a half hour before serving.

Makes 24

Vegetable pakoras

You can make bite-sized pakoras to serve hot as party finger food or as an entrée. Alternatively, form the mixture into large flattened fritters for a vegetarian main course. If you use hard vegetables such as potato, sweet potatoes, beans, carrots or peas, parcook them before you assemble the mixture.

2 cups finely diced mixed vegetables (fresh or frozen)
½ cup self-raising flour
½ cup chickpea flour (besan) or fine cornmeal
¾ teaspoon baking powder
1 teaspoon chilli powder
2 teaspoons garam masala or curry powder
½ teaspoon cracked black pepper
¾ teaspoon salt
2 eggs, beaten
about ½ cup water
oil for deep-frying

Dipping sauce
½–¾ cup tomato sauce (ketchup)
1–3 teaspoons tabasco or hot chilli sauce
2–3 teaspoons chopped coriander or parsley (optional)

Thaw frozen vegetables, if used. In a large mixing bowl combine the flours with the baking powder, spices and salt. Add the beaten eggs, with enough water to make a thick batter. Beat the mixture well, and leave for about 5 minutes while the baking powder activates.

Meanwhile, make the dipping sauce. Season the tomato sauce with tabasco or chilli sauce to taste, and stir in the chopped herbs. Spoon into a bowl suitable for dipping, or into individual sauce bowls if serving as a first or main course.

Heat oil for deep-frying, to medium-hot. Add the vegetables to the batter and stir well so everything is spread evenly. Use a spoon to scoop up walnut-sized quantities of the mixture and slide these into the oil. Fry until they are golden and bob to the surface, then allow another minute before retrieving them with a wire scoop. Drain on absorbent paper for a minute, then serve while still hot.

Makes about 40 tiny pakoras, or serves 6 as an entrée or light main course

Spicy sausage rolls

If you want to prepare everything ahead of time, the uncooked sausage rolls can be wrapped in plastic and frozen. Bake direct from the freezer, allowing about 30 minutes at 190°C (375°F).

2 sheets frozen puff pastry
grease and flour for the baking tray
400 g (13 oz) cubed beef, veal, chicken or pork
100 g (3½ oz) bacon, chopped
1 small onion, quartered
2 slices bread, soaked in cold water and drained
1 tablespoon garam masala
1¼ teaspoons salt
2–3 sprigs parsley or other herbs
2 tablespoons hot mango chutney
1 large egg, beaten
paprika

Set the pastry aside to thaw. Preheat the oven to 190°C (375°F). Lightly grease and flour a baking sheet.

Place the meat in a food processor fitted with the metal blade, chop finely and then remove. Put the bacon and onion in the processor and chop finely, then add the bread and the remaining ingredients except for the egg and paprika, and whiz again to mix. Return the meat and process once more until thoroughly mixed and reasonably smooth.

Cut each of the pastry sheets in half. Divide the meat mixture into four and form each portion into a sausage along the centre of a piece of pastry. Brush the edges with water, roll up and turn over so that the joins are on the underside. Lift carefully onto the prepared baking sheet. Brush the top of each roll with beaten egg and then dust lightly with paprika. Use a sharp knife to cut through each roll, making 6 small sausage rolls from each piece. Place in the centre of the preheated oven to cook for 20 minutes, until puffed, crisp and golden. Serve at once.

Makes 24 small rolls

Thai fish cakes

These are a knockout, and take no time at all when you purée the mixture in a food processor. Make small round balls for party food, or larger cakes for an entrée over shredded lettuce or in a curling leaf of Chinese cabbage (wombok).

400 g (13 oz) fish fillets, skinned and deboned
1 1/2 teaspoons Thai red curry paste
1 teaspoon bicarbonate of soda
1 egg white
1 1/2 tablespoons fish sauce
1/2 teaspoon salt
3 kaffir lime leaves, very, very finely chopped
salt and pepper
3 green beans, very, very finely sliced (optional)
oil for deep-frying

Cucumber chilli relish
2 tablespoons, very finely chopped continental cucumber (unpeeled)
1 teaspoon crushed garlic (optional)
1/4 cup white vinegar
1/4 cup fish sauce
1 1/2 tablespoons fine white sugar
chopped red chilli, to taste

Cut the fish fillets into chunks and place in a food processor with the curry paste, bicarbonate of soda, egg white, fish sauce and salt. Process to a very smooth paste, then add the lime leaves, salt and pepper, and process briefly. Lastly add the beans and process again briefly. With wet or oiled hands, shape the mixture as required: into small round balls or into larger balls flattened to about 12mm (1/2 in.) thick.

Combine the ingredients for the relish, heat for 2 minutes and set aside to cool.

Heat the oil in a wok or pan that is safe for deep-frying, and have ready a tray covered with paper towels. Fry the fish cakes, about 10 at a time, until golden-brown and floating on the surface. Remove with a wire scoop, and drain. Pierce with toothpicks and serve warm, with the relish in a shallow dish for dipping.

Makes about 30 small balls, or serves 4–6 as an entrée

Rice paper rolls

Delicious made with crunchy fresh prawns, but for a vegetarian snack you can substitute about 100 g (3½ oz) of shredded firm tofu. Guests could assemble their own rolls at the table, but if you choose to prepare the rolls yourself do so no more than a half hour before serving

60 g (2 oz) rice vermicelli, softened in hot water
12 medium-sized cooked prawns, peeled and deveined (optional)
1 small carrot, finely shredded or coarsely grated
½ cup fresh bean sprouts
½ cup shredded lettuce or shredded cucumber
Asian barbecue sauce or sweet chilli sauce
12 Vietnamese rice papers (*banh trang*), 22 cm diameter

Have the prepared ingredients ready on a plate. Fill a dish with lukewarm water and place a teatowel on the workbench. Dip a rice paper into the water, leaving it there long enough to soften (about 30 seconds). Lift out and place on the teatowel. Arrange a portion of each of the ingredients in the centre with a teaspoon of the sauce, fold the lower edge up, then fold in the two sides, and roll up. Proceed with the remainder. Serve with more of the sauce, for dipping.

Makes 12 rolls

Sweet potato wedges with tomato chilli chutney

Orange-fleshed sweet potatoes are best here, but you could use other kinds, or yams, potatoes or pumpkin. The chutney will keep for weeks in the refrigerator.

a 410-g (13½ oz) can whole peeled tomatoes, drained and chopped
up to ¼ cup fish sauce
⅓ cup sugar
1 teaspoon crushed garlic
1 teaspoon crushed ginger
3 teaspoons white vinegar
1 large fresh red chilli, chopped
1 teaspoon cornflour, blended in a little cold water
4 medium-sized sweet potatoes
2–3 cups vegetable oil
⅓–½ cup sour cream
sea salt
pepper

Note: the ¼ cup of fish sauce makes for a slightly salty chutney, ideal for the blandness of potatoes. Use less if you prefer.

Make the chutney first. In a small non-aluminium saucepan combine the tomatoes, fish sauce, sugar, garlic, ginger, vinegar and chilli. Bring to the boil, reduce heat to medium and simmer for about 20 minutes. Reduce heat a little further and cook for another 10 minutes or so: the chutney should be reasonably thick. Pour the cornflour mixture into the chutney and cook briefly to thicken, then remove from the heat and leave to cool.

Wash the sweet potatoes and cut them, unpeeled, into fingers of around 5 × 2.5 cm (2 × 1 in.). Boil in lightly salted water, or microwave with a splash of salted water, until half-cooked. Drain, and dry with paper towels.

Heat the oil in a large pan and fry the sweet-potato fingers until they are crisped on the surface and can be pierced easily with a skewer. Remove from the oil with a slotted spoon and drain briefly on paper towels. Pile onto a plate and season with flaky sea salt and some black pepper. Serve with the sour cream and chutney in separate bowls, for dipping.

Serves 4 or more as a snack or entrée

Chorizo empanadas

I discovered this easy little entertainer in Spain, home of the spicy chorizo sausage. The empanadas can be made with puff pastry, but bought shortcrust is a reasonable substitute for the lightly spiced and very buttery shortcrust used in Spain. You will need a 5-cm (2 in.) round pastry cutter.

1 large chorizo sausage (about 140 g or 5 oz)
375 g (12 oz) frozen shortcrust pastry
1 egg, beaten
3–4 semi-dried tomatoes, chopped
sprigs of thyme
8 black olives

Preheat the oven to 200°C (400°F). Cut the sausage into 24 slices, discarding the ends. Roll out the pastry very thinly and cut into 2, making one piece just slightly larger than the other. Brush the smaller piece of pastry with some of the beaten egg, then arrange the sausage slices over it, leaving about 1.5 cm (¾ in) between each slice. On each slice of sausage place a small piece of tomato and a few thyme leaves. Cover with the larger piece of pastry, pressing down around the sausage pieces. Brush the top of the pastry with the remaining egg and then use the cutter to cut out each empanada, keeping the sausage filling in the middle.

With a spatula lift the empanadas onto a lightly floured baking sheet. Cut the olives into small pieces and place a few on each empanada. Put in the hot oven and cook for about 10 minutes, until golden-brown. Serve at once.

Makes 24

Crunch with punch

Ikan bilis are dried and salted miniature anchovies readily available from Asian shops. Fried crisp and then tossed in a wok with salted peanuts and spices, they make a delightful crunchy nibble to go with drinks. The mix can also be sprinkled over noodles, curries, rice or vegetable dishes.

1 cup dried ikan bilis
1 cup salted peanuts
2 cups peanut or vegetable oil
1 tablespoon sesame oil
3 large garlic cloves, peeled and sliced
1 teaspoon chilli flakes or powder
1½ teaspoons salt
1 teaspoon cumin seeds

Rinse, drain and dry the ikan bilis and peanuts. Heat the oils and cook the garlic until it begins to colour. Remove the garlic and discard. Increase the heat to high and fry the ikan bilis for about 40 seconds, then remove and drain on paper towels. Pour away the oil, wipe out the pan and reheat to medium. Return the ikan bilis, and add the remaining ingredients. Stir well for about 40 seconds, then remove from the heat and leave to cool. What is not eaten on the day can be stored in an airtight container for about 10 days. Reheat briefly in the microwave oven and cool a little before serving.

Hot potatoes

These make easy and economical catering for a crowd, but are equally delicious as a vegetarian dish or beside a steak or grill.

12 medium-sized new potatoes
a little salted water
2 slices rindless bacon, finely chopped
1 medium onion, very finely chopped
1 tablespoon olive oil
a little chilli oil (page 142)
1 cup sour cream
2 tablespoons sweet chilli sauce
1 tablespoon chopped coriander, parsley or chives

Cut the potatoes in half and place them, cut side up, in a flat microwave dish. Sprinkle with a few tablespoons of salted water and microwave on High for 6 minutes. Test, and cook longer if needed. (If you don't have a microwave, boil the whole potatoes in lightly salted water until they can be pierced easily with a sharp knife. Drain, and cut in half.) Cover the potatoes with foil to keep them warm.

Meanwhile, sauté the bacon and onion in the oil with a few shakes of chilli oil, until crisp. Stir almost constantly so they cook evenly.

To serve, arrange the potatoes on a platter and top each with a dollop of sour cream and chilli sauce, a sprinkle of herbs and the fried bacon and onion.

Makes 24 pieces

Hot shots

Afrodisiac

Prepare a potent bloody Mary with tomato or vegetable juice, tequila instead of vodka (or use a mixture of both), a splash of Worcestershire sauce and a big squeeze of lime or lemon. Shake over ice. Place a large fresh oyster in each shot glass, top with the bloody Mary mix and shake in a dash of tabasco or chilli oil.

Red-hot Mary

If you can find a bottle of pepper-flavoured vodka, keep one in the freezer. Or make your own, by adding sprigs of fresh green peppercorns, a tablespoon of white peppercorns or mixed peppercorns and a small crushed dried chilli to a bottle of vodka. It will need a week or two for the peppery flavour to develop.

1 cup tomato juice
2 shots pepper vodka
$\frac{1}{2}$–1 teaspoon tabasco
a big pinch of celery salt (or salt and a sprinkle of celery seeds)
lime or lemon juice, to taste
ice cubes
$\frac{1}{2}$ celery stalk (with leaves), slit lengthwise

Place everything except the ice cubes and celery in a cocktail shaker or screwtop jar, and shake to blend well. Pour into long glasses, over ice, and pop in a celery stick.

Serves 2

Pot Boilers

IF I CAN'T HAVE GOOD MUSIC, a glass of red wine and my nearest and dearest at my side when I curl up on the couch in front of a winter fire, I'll settle for a purring cat on my lap, a good book and a bowl of soup. In the colder months, soups are comfort food personified. And there is added satisfaction when chillies or pepper are brought into the equation.

This is not to say that soup should be off the menu in summer. Like a steaming cup of tea, chilli-hot soup acts as a diaphoretic, nature's own climate control for the body, by inducing a healthy and cooling burst of perspiration. This certainly works in Thailand, where soups like their *tom yum* are blisteringly hot and startlingly tart. And I find that taking the liberty of lavishing chillies into a gazpacho or fish soup takes these classics into an exciting new taste arena.

Baked breads are a natural companion for soup, but the muffins and hotcakes I've included here can also star independently, as a morning or afternoon snack or breakfast with a bite.

Tom yum gung

Thailand's distinctive prawn soup takes barely 5 minutes if you use a stock made from Japanese instant dashi granules. They have, I think, a deeper flavour and are less salty than most commercial fish stocks.

4 cups boiling water
2–3 teaspoons dashi stock granules
12 large fresh prawns (peeled or unpeeled, as you prefer)
1 lemongrass stalk, diagonally sliced
4 kaffir lime leaves (optional)
4 mild red chillies, halved lengthwise (de-seeded if preferred)
2 roma tomatoes, quartered lengthwise
1 spring onion, diagonally sliced
2 tablespoons fish sauce
1 teaspoon sugar
2 tablespoons lime or lemon juice

Pour the boiling water over 2 teaspoons of the stock granules in a medium-sized saucepan and check for flavour, adding more granules if needed. Put in the prawns, lemongrass, lime leaves, chillies and tomatoes. Bring to the boil, reduce heat and simmer for 2 minutes. Add spring onion, fish sauce, sugar and lime juice, and check for salt. Serve in deep bowls, perhaps with a stalk of lemongrass for stirring through.

Gazpacho with a kick

I like to leave this for a few hours or even overnight in the fridge so that the flavours develop and the soup gets really cold.

1 kg (2 lb) well-ripened tomatoes
1 large mild red chilli, de-seeded and roughly chopped
1 large green chilli, de-seeded and roughly chopped
2–3 spring onions, trimmed and roughly chopped
2–4 sprigs parsley or coriander
2–3 sprigs marjoram or oregano
2–3 sprigs dill or basil
1 medium cucumber (about 100 g or 3½ oz), unpeeled but de-seeded and chopped
½ green capsicum, finely chopped
1 cup iced water or vegetable stock
1 tablespoon red-wine vinegar
salt and pepper to taste
extra-virgin olive oil (optional)

Halve the tomatoes and squeeze out the seeds. Slice flesh thinly and place in a food processor fitted with the metal blade. Using the pulse control, chop the tomatoes to a coarse purée, which will take about 12 one-second bursts. Pour into a bowl.

Place the chillies, onions and herbs in the food processor and again use the pulse control to chop them reasonably finely. Add ½ cup of the tomato purée, process briefly and then pour this mixture over the remaining tomato. Add the remaining ingredients except the oil, and mix well. Chill, or ladle straight into bowls and serve over ice.

Serves 6

 Make a delicious light-green stock for this soup: simmer diced giant white radish (daikon), chopped onion, spinach leaves, basil stalks and parsley stalks in water for 20 minutes. Strain before use.

Korean chilli soup

A time-bomb of a soup in Korea, but I have given a milder version. It is traditionally a rich beef soup made from stock bones, with slivers of beef to counteract its red-hot chilli heat. For this version, you can use either beef or chicken stock: tetrapack stocks are better than a cube or powder.

1 tablespoon sesame oil
1 medium onion, finely sliced
200 g (6½ oz) coarsely minced beef or chicken
1 tablespoon sesame seeds
½–1½ teaspoons crushed garlic
2–3 teaspoons chilli powder or chilli sauce
2 teaspoons ground sweet paprika
1 tablespoon light soy sauce
4 cups beef or chicken stock
salt and pepper
1 spring onion, chopped
140 g (5 oz) fresh bean sprouts, blanched briefly and drained

In a saucepan heat the sesame oil over medium–high heat and sauté the onion for about 2 minutes, until reasonably well cooked. Add the minced beef or chicken and stir-fry for about 1½ minutes; the bottom of the saucepan will become quite browned, which will give colour and flavour to the soup. Add the sesame seeds, garlic, chilli, paprika and soy sauce, and cook for about 30 seconds, stirring. Add the stock and bring quickly to the boil, then reduce the heat and simmer for about 8 minutes. Season to taste with salt and pepper.

Divide the spring onion and bean sprouts between four bowls and pour the soup over.

Serves 4

Sweet potato, corn and chilli soup

Being a sweet-potato devotee, I use them as often as possible. In this soup I sometimes use both the orange- and the white-fleshed (pink-skinned) varieties. The orange ones have a delightful colour and a creamy texture, so I purée them and dice the slightly more starchy white ones to give the soup texture.

600 g (1 1/4 lb) orange sweet potatoes
3 cups water or chicken stock
1 medium onion, finely chopped
1 large mild green chilli, de-seeded and sliced
1 large mild red chilli, de-seeded and sliced
2 tablespoons butter or olive oil
140 g (5 oz) corn kernels (or peas)
1 teaspoon sweet paprika
salt and pepper
1/2 cup sour cream

Peel and cube the sweet potatoes. Boil in lightly salted water until tender enough to mash (about 16 minutes) and then drain, reserving the liquid. To microwave, place the cubed sweet potatoes in a microwave dish with 2 tablespoons of the stock or water, cover and microwave on High for 6 minutes.

In a medium-sized saucepan sauté the onion and chillies in the butter or oil until softened. Add half the water or stock, the corn or peas and the paprika. Bring to the boil and simmer until the vegetables are tender (about 6 minutes).

Transfer the cooked sweet potato to a food processor and process with the remaining water or stock until smooth. Pour over the mixture in the saucepan, simmer for 1–2 minutes, then add salt and pepper to taste. Ladle into bowls, add a swirl of sour cream and serve hot with crusty bread or garlic toast.

Serves 4

Peppery potato and rocket soup

I love the effect peppery rocket has in a bland potato soup. Rocket is easy to grow and I have had success planting the roots from a hydroponic punnet after harvesting its leaves.

600 g (1 1/4 lb) new potatoes, peeled
1 fresh green chilli, de-seeded and chopped
4 cups chicken or vegetable stock
4 bunches (about 500 g or 1 lb) rocket, rinsed and roughly chopped
salt and black pepper
2 tablespoons chopped parsley
rocket pesto or sambal ulek (optional)

Cut the potatoes into dice and place in a saucepan with the chilli and half the stock. Bring to the boil and simmer for 10 minutes. Add half the rocket with the salt and pepper, and bring to the boil again. Simmer for a further 10 minutes, by which time the potato should have begun to break up. Transfer to a food processor and process briefly, then add the remaining rocket and the parsley. Process again to purée, but retain some texture. Return the purée to the saucepan and add enough of the remaining stock to make a thick and creamy soup. Check seasoning and simmer briefly to heat.

Serve in large soup bowls and swirl on a little rocket pesto or sambal ulek. For added punch, spread toasted crostini with chilli butter (page 145), cover with grated parmesan and pop under a hot grill for a few minutes. Serve beside, or floated on top of, the soup.

Serves 4

Chunky curry fish soup

I keep individually wrapped skinless fish fillets in the freezer. They thaw in a few minutes, though for a dish like this I don't even wait for them to thaw but put them in frozen and cook everything for an extra minute or two. To make a satisfying main course, increase the quantity of stock and add finely diced cucumber, zucchini or celery, or a handful of spinach leaves or bean sprouts, and pre-softened rice noodles.

200 g (6½ oz) diced white fish
2 spring onions, chopped
1 cup coconut milk
1 cup fish stock, or water and a fish-stock cube
¾ cup chopped canned tomatoes
1 large chilli, de-seeded and sliced (optional)
1 teaspoon crushed ginger
½ teaspoon black pepper
1 tablespoon curry powder
salt to taste
chopped dill, coriander or basil for garnish

Cut the fish into 1.5-cm (¾ in.) cubes. Place everything except the herbs in a saucepan (preferably not an aluminium one) and simmer for 5–6 minutes. Ladle into soup bowls, sprinkle herbs over and serve with toasted baguette slices spread with cayenne butter (page 145).

Serves 2–3

Chinese sour and hot soup

I have modified the flavour of this traditionally hot and tart soup. Your guests may enjoy extra seasoning: prepare a small tray bearing bowls of vinegar, chilli oil, chopped coriander and chopped spring onions, so people can help themselves.

5 cups chicken stock
½ cup sliced dried shiitake mushrooms or wood-ear fungus
1½ tablespoons light soy sauce
1 teaspoon crushed ginger
1 fresh red chilli, de-seeded and chopped
100 g (3½ oz) chicken or pork, finely shredded
100 g (3½ oz) tofu, diced
½ cup shredded bamboo shoot
½ cup straw mushrooms, sliced
3 spring onions, chopped
2 tablespoons Chinese black vinegar, or sherry or balsamic vinegar
1 teaspoon chilli bean paste or hot chilli sauce
salt and white pepper
1½ tablespoons cornflour
2 tablespoons water
2 eggs, lightly beaten

In a non-aluminium saucepan combine the stock, dried mushrooms, soy sauce, ginger and chilli, and bring to the boil. Simmer for about 10 minutes. Add the chicken or pork, tofu, bamboo shoot, straw mushrooms and the white parts of the spring onions, and simmer again briefly. Season with the vinegar and chilli paste or sauce, and salt and pepper to taste.

Blend the cornflour with the water. While the soup is bubbling, stir in the cornflour mixture and continue to stir slowly until the sauce thickens slightly and becomes somewhat translucent. At this stage, just before serving, drizzle the beaten eggs into the soup in a slow stream, allowing it to set without stirring. Add the spring-onion greens, check seasoning again and then serve.

Serves 4

Gumbo

Gumbo, a star feature of Cajun-Creole cooking, is a chunky rice-based stew that is eaten from deep bowls with fingers and a spoon. I have decreased the rice to make a hearty soup. *File* is powdered dried sassafras leaves, used as a thickener by the American Indians; it has an unusual taste and viscosity. Some delis may stock it, but the soup will survive without it.

½ cup long-grain rice
7 cups chicken stock
1 large onion, chopped
¾ cup chopped green capsicum
¾ cup chopped celery
¾ cup sliced okra or eggplant
2 small unripe tomatoes, chopped
3 slices of bacon, chopped
3 tablespoons butter
1½ teaspoons crushed garlic
2½ tablespoons plain flour
1 cup canned crushed tomatoes
2 bay leaves
1 teaspoon dried mixed herbs
2 teaspoons chilli powder or sauce
salt and pepper
1 cup cooked chicken, diced
1 cup small cooked prawns
1 tablespoon *file* powder (optional)

In a medium–large saucepan stir the rice into the chicken stock. Bring to the boil, reduce heat and simmer gently for about 25 minutes, until the rice is mushy.

In another pan, sauté the onion, capsicum, celery, okra or eggplant, unripe tomatoes and bacon in the butter for about 8 minutes until well cooked, adding the garlic after the first 5 minutes. Scatter the flour over the ingredients and stir it in, then add the crushed tomatoes, bay leaves, herbs, chilli, salt and pepper and bring briskly to the boil. Add the cooked rice, simmer for 5 minutes, then add the chicken and prawns, and the *file* if used. Stir to heat through, then serve.

Serves 6

Red pepper muffins

These make a lively accompaniment to soups, salads or a cheese platter. If you cannot find pickled red chillies, you can substitute 1½ teaspoons hot chilli sauce or a chilli paste such as sambal ulek.

2 cups self-raising flour
1½ teaspoons baking powder
2 teaspoons salt
¾ teaspoon sweet paprika
1 large egg
¼ cup vegetable or olive oil
1 cup buttermilk or milk (more if needed)
2½ teaspoons finely chopped pickled red chillies

Preheat the oven to 200°C (400°F). Sift the flour, baking powder, salt and paprika into a bowl. Stir in the egg, oil and buttermilk or milk, the chopped chillies and as much extra milk as you need to make a soft batter; do not overbeat. Spoon into greased muffin tins and bake in the preheated oven for 12–18 minutes. Test by inserting a skewer into the centre of a muffin: it should come out clean.

Remove the muffins from the tins to a cake cooling rack and allow to cool a little before serving. They can be reheated in a microwave.

Makes 18 small or 12 large muffins

 This recipe also makes a great chilli-cheese bread. Add ½ cup grated cheese and some chopped herbs to the dough, pat out on a floured baking sheet, spread on more cheese and bake for 15–28 minutes.

Cajun hotcakes

Fabulous with soup or just on their own, dripping with butter. They are also a delicious made-in-minutes alternative to traditional Indian breads when you serve a curry, in which case you can omit the cheese or replace it with 2 tablespoons of chopped parsley or coriander. And for a chilli fiends' Devonshire tea, split hot-from-the-oven hotcakes and serve with tomato chilli chutney (page 23) and a creamy mix of spreadable cream cheese whipped with sour cream.

3 cups self-raising flour
1 teaspoon salt
2½ teaspoons cajun seasoning
1½ teaspoons baking powder
1½ cups luke-warm milk
1 cup grated cheese
extra flour

Preheat the oven to 220°C (425°F). Sift the flour, salt, cajun seasoning and baking powder into a mixing bowl and make a well in the centre. Add most of the milk and all of the cheese, and work lightly into the flour: the dough should be quite soft, but not sticky. Add the remaining milk if needed.

On a lightly floured work surface, gently press out the dough to a thickness of 1.5 cm (¾ in.). Cut into 20 portions, using a 5-cm (2 in.) round cutter, and place the rounds side by side on a floured baking sheet. Moisten the tops of the hotcakes with the remaining milk and bake in the centre of the preheated oven for about 12 minutes, until lightly browned on top. To test if the hotcakes are done, pierce one with a skewer: it should come out dry. Serve warm with butter.

Makes 18–20

Light Bites

TRADITIONAL MEAL STRUCTURES have been challenged by our infatuation for lighter dishes and a wider range of taste sensations. It makes healthy sense to graze on middle-sized dishes with a variety of ingredients: they are easy on the digestive system and help to ensure a balanced intake of vitamins and minerals.

Middle-sized dishes also give you the chance to experiment with new ingredients, sauces and cooking styles. And they challenge the cook to be creative about presentation. Aim for height when you assemble these meals on the plate. Make colour and texture contrasts work, and garnishes interesting. Use sprigs of fresh chillies and peppercorns, and maintain a herb garden, even if it is just a few pots on a window ledge or balcony, so you can finish your dishes with vibrantly fresh herbs.

Satisfy questing palates with flexible menus of the dishes that follow. They are versatile dishes which can be served on their own or mixed and matched as separate courses. They are perfect for light and lively lunches, are impressive on the dinner table, and are not too heavy as a late-night meal.

Carpaccio with Asian flavours

You'll find Chinese black vinegar at Asian food stores. If you can't, use balsamic vinegar instead.

315 g (10 oz) best-quality rump or fillet steak, in a piece
1 large garlic clove, very finely chopped
1 tablespoon pickled ginger, very finely chopped
1 small red onion, very finely chopped
1 fresh green chilli, de-seeded and very finely chopped
1½ tablespoons very finely chopped coriander or basil
3 teaspoons sesame oil
2 tablespoons light olive or vegetable oil
3 teaspoons Chinese black vinegar (or balsamic vinegar)
½ teaspoon Sichuan peppercorns, crushed
salt

Place the beef in the freezer, wrapped in plastic wrap, for at least 40 minutes. It needs to become firm enough to be sliced so thin you could read through it. Serve the beef on large individual plates, overlapping the slices, or arranged as the mood strikes.

In a small mixing bowl combine the garlic, ginger, onion, chilli and coriander or basil. Scatter evenly over the beef, then drizzle with the oils and vinegar. Season and serve, perhaps with extra slices of pickled ginger for ginger-lovers. You can also provide grissini sticks on which guests can wrap their meat slices.

Serves 4

Frittata of peppered pancetta with spinach

It is a good idea to keep one pan just for omelettes and their Mediterranean alter egos, frittatas and tortillas. Treat it like a wok: after washing with detergent and a soft brush, rinse and dry, then rub with oiled kitchen paper. This way you can maintain a smooth inner surface that allows you to slide out the omelette without it catching.

6 eggs
1 1/2 tablespoons grated parmesan
salt and pepper
2 teaspoons chopped parsley (optional)
3/4 cup very finely diced peppered pancetta
2 1/2 tablespoons olive oil
1 tightly packed cup young spinach leaves, rinsed and dried
chilli oil or tabasco (optional)

In a bowl beat the eggs lightly with the parmesan, salt, pepper and parsley. Set aside.

Preheat the oven to 220°C (425°F). Heat an iron pan with an ovenproof handle: if you don't have one, use an iron or non-stick pan and heat the griller instead. Pour half the oil into the hot pan and sauté the pancetta for about 1 1/2 minutes, until crisped. (Instead of the pancetta, you could use 3/4 cup chopped prosciutto or other ham, plus a chopped fresh chilli.) Add the remaining oil and arrange the pancetta and the spinach evenly across the bottom of the pan. When the oil is very hot, carefully pour in the eggs without disturbing the other ingredients. Use a spoon to push the spinach leaves beneath the surface of the egg. Cook for about 30 seconds over high heat, then reduce to medium and cook for about a minute, to set and brown the base. Brown the top in the oven or under the griller for about 5 minutes. Sprinkle with a little chilli oil or tabasco (if used), cut the frittata in half and serve at once on warmed plates.

Serves 2–3

Nam tok (Thai beef salad)

Anyone who has travelled in Thailand's far north-east will probably have encountered *nam tok*. And chances are it was made with steaks of young buffalo. It is quite a sensation if you replace the beef with grilled duck breast, left beautifully rare, or chicken breast (preferably with the skin left on for extra flavour and succulence).

1 tablespoon fish sauce
⅓ teaspoon salt
½ teaspoon cracked black pepper
2 teaspoons Thai red curry paste
light olive or vegetable oil
2 fillet or sirloin steaks, or a large rump steak (about 350 g or 11 oz in all)
4 handfuls of young curly endive
½ punnet snow-pea sprouts
½ cup sliced red onion
¼ cup (loosely packed) mint, basil or coriander leaves
1½ teaspoons sugar
2 tablespoons freshly squeezed lime juice
1 tablespoon very finely shredded red chilli
1 tablespoon chopped roasted peanuts

Make a paste of the fish sauce, salt, pepper, curry paste and a little oil, and brush it evenly over the steaks.

Heat a ribbed iron pan, a barbecue grill or a heavy frying pan, and moisten the surface using a paper towel dipped in oil. Sear the steaks over high heat, cooking them well on the surface but leaving the inside rare. Set aside for 4–5 minutes to rest, before cutting into thin slices.

Combine the endive, snow peas, onions and most of the herb leaves and moisten with a little oil. Pile some of this salad in the centre of each plate and drape the sliced meat over. Stir the sugar into the lime juice, and once dissolved pour it over the salad. Garnish with the chillies, peanuts and remaining mint before serving.

Serves 4 as an entrée, or 2 as a main course

Chicken in tahini sauce over chilled noodles

This Chinese–Japanese dish is constructed in a flash if you have a roast chicken on hand, and only needs an extra 10 minutes if you have to cook the chicken. It looks perfect on square oriental plates. For a vegetarian variation, grill tofu until golden, shred with a sharp knife and use instead of the chicken.

250 g (8 oz) boneless roast chicken, or 2 skinless chicken breast fillets
3 bundles instant egg noodles (or buckwheat noodles if preferred)
2 spring onions, chopped
1–2 celery stalks, finely sliced on the diagonal
$\frac{1}{2}$ cup tahini
$\frac{1}{2}$ cup cold water
3 tablespoons rice vinegar
1 teaspoon salt
1–1$\frac{1}{2}$ teaspoons hot chilli sauce
sesame seeds (optional)

Skin the roast chicken, if used, tear the meat into thin strips, cover and set aside. If using chicken fillets, heat a cast-iron or non-stick pan, moisten with oil and cook the breasts turning two or three times, until cooked through (about 7 minutes in all). Remove from the heat and leave to cool.

Cook the noodles in unsalted water for about 2$\frac{1}{2}$ minutes (buckwheat noodles may take a little longer), until *al dente*. Drain and then cover with cold water to prevent them overcooking. Drain well, and mix with the shallots, celery and chicken.

In a mixing bowl, beat the tahini, water and vinegar together until creamy and season with salt and chilli sauce. Taste, and add more vinegar if you like. Pour over the noodles and toss to mix well. Pile the salad onto plates and scatter with sesame seeds, if used.

The salad and the dressing can be prepared up to 2 hours in advance and kept covered (separately) in the refrigerator until needed. Beat up the sauce, add water to thin it if required, and mix into the salad just before serving. Any excess sauce makes an excellent dressing for other salads.

Serves 2 as a main course, or 4 as an entrée

Pissaladière

Serve this Provençale pizza with salad leaves moistened with olive oil and balsamic vinegar. It is also an appealing party food, cut into thick fingers and served warm. If you do not have frozen pastry, use thickly sliced Italian bread or make up a soft scone dough which you press into a rectangle and bake for 8 minutes before adding the toppings.

1 sheet frozen puff pastry
6 semi-dried tomato pieces, chopped
1 cup oil-marinated grilled eggplant, chopped
1 large fresh red chilli, de-seeded and chopped (or 2 pickled chillies, chopped)
12 small black olives or stuffed green olives
½ cup feta, crumbled
¾ teaspoon dried mixed herbs
salt and black pepper
milk (optional)

Cut the pastry sheet in half, moisten the top surface of one piece lightly with water and press the other sheet on top. Using the edge of a knife blade, hit gently along the edges of the pastry, keeping the knife horizontal to the pastry: this encourages the layers to separate and puff during cooking. Then, with the point of the knife, score a line around the top of the pastry, about 12 mm (½ in.) from the edge. Place the pastry on a lightly greased and floured baking sheet, and refrigerate.

Preheat the oven to 220°C (400°F). Spread the tomatoes and eggplant evenly over the pastry, inside the scored line. Scatter the chilli, olives, cheese and herbs evenly over, and season with salt and pepper. Brush the empty border of the pastry with milk, if you like, to help it colour during baking. Cook in the preheated oven for about 15 minutes, until the pastry is well risen and golden, and the cheese melting. Cut in half and serve hot or cold.

Serves 2

▶

From the top: Sweet potato wedges (page 23), Green olive and chilli tapenade (page 10) served on bruschetta, and Tomato chilli chutney (page 23)

Chillied chicken and avocado cheese toast

This is one of the best ways to use up day-old focaccia, and it is almost as delicious if you leave out the chicken. I have an iron barbecue plate with one half ribbed and the other flat: it fits over two gas rings on my stove, giving plenty of cooking surface for this family favourite.

4 wedges focaccia
4 chicken thigh fillets
salt and pepper
chilli oil (page 142) or olive oil
4 large slices rindless bacon
2 tablespoons red-pepper jam (page 143) or 3 tablespoons hot fruit chutney, mashed
2 avocadoes, mashed and seasoned
about 250 g (8 oz) very thinly sliced melting cheese (e.g. mozzarella, cheddar)

Heat a ribbed iron pan and a flat pan to hot, then reduce heat to medium.

Slit the focaccia wedges in half and set aside. Butterfly the chicken fillets to make rectangular pieces of even thickness. Season with salt and pepper, and brush lightly with oil, then place on the ribbed pan to cook for about 7 minutes, turning twice. At the same time, cook the bacon in the flat pan until crisped.

Preheat a grill to hot or an oven to 200°C (400°F). Remove the cooked chicken to a warmed plate and place the focaccia pieces, cut side down, in the ribbed pan to toast.

Spread red-pepper jam or chutney on the toasted side of the four base pieces of focaccia, then layer with the chicken, bacon and mashed avocado. Top with the cheese, set on a baking tray and place under the grill or in the oven until the cheese melts. Season with cracked black pepper, position the toasted focaccia tops in place, and serve at once.

Serves 4

◀

A peppery potato and rocket soup (page 35)
and Tom yum gung (page 31)

Cajun chicken salad

Pickled garlic and leeks can be purchased from Asian stores. You could use half a punnet of snow-pea shoots instead of the witloof.

350 g (11 oz) chicken thigh fillets
1 tablespoon honey
1 tablespoon cajun seasoning
1 teaspoon salt
2 teaspoons cracked black pepper (optional)
2 tablespoons very fine polenta, ground almonds or dry breadcrumbs
1½ tablespoons vegetable oil or olive oil
4 handfuls small-leaved lettuce or rocket
1 head witloof, leaves separated (optional)
1 small continental cucumber (unpeeled), finely sliced
1 large red chilli, de-seeded and very finely sliced
coriander sprigs (optional)
vinaigrette dressing, or olive oil and lemon juice
small pickled onions, garlic or leeks, drained (optional)

The chicken cooks best if it is of even thickness. Unroll fillets, place inside upwards on a cutting board and butterfly by slicing into the thickest parts, beginning at the centre and working outwards. Do not sever the cut pieces, but fold outwards, and gently bat with a rolling pin to give rectangular pieces. Pat dry with paper towels.

Make a paste of the honey, cajun seasoning, salt and pepper, and spread it over the chicken. If time allows, cover with a cloth and leave for 15 minutes. Coat lightly with the polenta, almonds or breadcrumbs.

Heat a non-stick pan to medium and moisten with the oil. Put in the chicken fillets and cook for about 3½ minutes on each side. Remove to a plate and leave to cool.

Arrange lettuce, witloof and cucumber on 4 plates. Add a few pieces of chilli and coriander to each, and pour dressing over. Cut the chicken into thick fingers and drape over the salad. Scatter with the pickled vegetables before serving.

Serves 6 as an entrée, and 4 as a small main course

Teriyaki scallops on soba noodles

Cubes of white fish, shelled prawns or very small whole cleaned octopus or squid could replace the scallops, which seem to have become rather expensive of late.

3 spring onions
12 large snow peas (or 1 punnet snow-pea sprouts)
1 fresh red chilli
250 g (8 oz) dried buckwheat (soba) noodles
1 teaspoon crushed Sichuan peppercorns or black pepper
1 tablespoon sesame oil
3 tablespoons butter
315 g (10 oz) fresh scallops, preferably with the orange roe attached
¾ cup teriyaki marinade
1½ tablespoons lemon juice

Trim the spring onions, cut into 5-cm (2 in.) lengths and then shred finely lengthwise. If using snow peas, string them and cut diagonally in half; for snow-pea sprouts, trim the cut ends and rinse the sprouts in cold water. De-seed and finely shred the chilli.

Bring a saucepan of unsalted water to the boil. Add the noodles, and when the water comes again to a boil add ½ cup cold water. Repeat this process once more and when the water is boiling again reduce the heat to medium and simmer the noodles for about 3 minutes. (It is important not to overcook buckwheat noodles, as they collapse.) Drain the noodles and place them in a bowl with the pepper and sesame oil. Mix well, using two forks.

Heat the butter in a non-stick pan and quickly sauté the onions and scallops until the former wilt and the latter firm up and turn white (about 1½ minutes). Add the snow peas or sprouts, the chilli and ¼ cup of the teriyaki marinade and bubble briskly to reduce it slightly. Add lemon juice to taste, then tip into a bowl and set aside.

Bring the remaining teriyaki sauce to a boil in the same pan, add the noodles and toss until the sauce is absorbed. Return the scallop mixture and warm through. Mound high on four plates, using tongs to arrange the scallop and pea mixture over the top. Serve at once.

Serves 4

Chilli chicken turnovers

Our local Vietnamese baker does pork turnovers to perfection and my daughter finds them irresistible. For this version, you can use chicken or pork.

2 sheets frozen puff pastry
butter and flour for the baking sheet
2 large garlic cloves, peeled
1 large green chilli, de-seeded and roughly chopped
2–3 sprigs coriander, roughly chopped
2 spring onions, chopped
½ cup water chestnuts, drained
600 g (13 oz) minced chicken or pork
2 eggs
1 teaspoon salt
1 teaspoon white pepper or chilli oil (page 142)
sesame seeds (optional)
sweet chilli sauce or hot chutney, for serving

Preheat the oven to 190°C (375°F). Set the pastry aside to thaw. Lightly butter and flour a baking sheet.

Place the garlic, chilli and coriander in a food processor and chop finely. Add the shallots and water chestnuts, and chop briefly. Add the chicken or pork, 1 whole egg and the white of another, the salt and the pepper. Chop briefly, using the pulse control.

Cut each pastry sheet into 4 squares. Place a portion of the filling in the centre of each square and fold the pastry over diagonally to make triangular turnovers. Press a fork around the joined edges to seal. Brush with the remaining egg yolk, lightly beaten and sprinkle with sesame seeds, if used. Place the pastries on the prepared baking sheet and bake in the preheated oven for about 25 minutes, until golden-brown and cooked through.

Serve hot or cold, with sweet chilli sauce or hot chutney.

Makes 8

Tomato bruschetta with peppered pancetta

If semi-dried tomatoes are too expensive, or if you have none on hand and have a few hours to spare, why not make your own? Simply slice fresh roma tomatoes in half lengthwise, arrange in an oven tray, season with olive oil, salt, pepper and mixed dried herbs, and place in a very low oven (about 120°C or 250°F) for about 3 hours until they collapse.

8 slices ciabatta or other Italian bread, or sourdough
3 tablespoons pesto
16 very thin slices peppered pancetta
1½ cups chopped semi-dried tomatoes
24 large basil leaves
salt and pepper

Toast the bread on one side under a hot grill. Spread pesto on the untoasted side, add semi-dried tomatoes, basil, salt and pepper, and top with the pancetta. Return to the hot grill briefly, until the pancetta has crisped slightly. Serve at once.

Serves 4

Lamburgers with harissa mayonnaise

Most supermarkets sell minced lamb. It makes delicious burger patties, especially when tricked up with the Middle Eastern seasonings that go so well with lamb.

1 medium onion, roughly chopped

4–5 large sprigs parsley or mint, stems removed

1 large garlic clove, peeled

1½ teaspoons ground cumin

¾ teaspoon allspice

1 teaspoon salt

600 g (1¼ lb) minced lamb

½ cup crumbled pita or Italian bread, soaked in milk

1 large egg

1½–2 tablespoons olive oil or vegetable oil

1½ teaspoons harissa or other hot chilli paste

3 tablespoons mayonnaise

2 teaspoons sesame oil (optional)

4 hamburger buns

4 lettuce leaves

2 large ripe tomatoes, thickly sliced

1 small continental cucumber, sliced, or 8 slices dill pickle

In a large food-processor bowl combine the onion, herbs and garlic, and chop finely. Add the spices and salt, and process briefly. Add the lamb and process again, using the pulse control, until well mixed. Lastly add the drained and squeezed bread and the egg, and process once more. Shape into 4 large patties using wet hands.

Heat the oils in a large pan and over medium heat cook the patties until they are well browned on the underside (about 3 minutes). Turn, and cook on the other side for about 5 minutes, then turn again and cook until done (another 3–5 minutes). Meanwhile, beat the harissa or chilli paste into the mayonnaise.

To assemble the lamburgers, slit open the buns, butter them if you like, and layer each with lettuce, a meat patty, sliced tomatoes, and cucumber or dill. Spread with the harissa mayonnaise, cover with the other half of the bun, and serve at once.

Makes 4

Garlic chilli prawns

An indulgence, but what a delicious one! And particularly impressive if you present the prawns in small heatproof dishes that you have warmed in the oven (place them on saucers or mats to protect the table). Serve with plain or garlic bread.

20 medium-sized green prawns (about 375 g or 12 oz), shelled but with tails intact
3 tablespoons olive oil
2 tablespoons butter
1½ teaspoons crushed garlic
½ teaspoon crushed red chilli
½ teaspoon cracked black pepper
salt to taste
2–3 teaspoons chopped parsley

Rinse the prawns and dry on paper towels. Heat the oil and butter in a wok or non-stick frying pan. Sauté the prawns for about 2½ minutes until they change colour. Add the garlic, chilli and black pepper, and cook, stirring the prawns constantly, until they are firm (about 1 minute more). Season with salt, stir in the parsley, and serve at once.

Serves 4

Chicken laab

This delightfully herbaceous salad features white chicken, which has been stir-fried without oil. If you use a roast chicken (skinned, de-boned and coarsely minced in a food processor) you can assemble the dish very quickly.

315 g (11 oz) minced chicken
1 medium red onion
1½ cups mixed fresh herb leaves (basil, coriander and mint)
2 tablespoons fish sauce
2 tablespoons lime juice
1–2 teaspoons chilli flakes, or to taste
2 teaspoons sugar
1–2 tablespoons fried onion flakes (optional)
4 crinkly-edged Chinese cabbage or lettuce leaves
crushed roasted peanuts, or toasted pine nuts

Heat a wok or non-stick pan over medium–high heat and stir the chicken without oil: keep it constantly moving and turning as it cooks, so it does not stick. Do not allow it to colour. Remove from the pan and allow to cool.

Cut the onion into slim wedges, separating the layers. In a small bowl whisk together the fish sauce, lime juice, chilli and sugar. Pour over the cooled chicken and mix well, then add the fried onion (if used) and half of the red onion pieces and herbs. Mix well again.

Place a cabbage or lettuce leaf on each plate, divide the remaining herbs and red onion pieces over the leaves, then top with the prepared chicken salad. Scatter with the peanuts or pine nuts and serve.

Serves 4

African chicken livers

Serve wrapped in burrito tortillas, on toasted bruschetta or in warmed, hollowed brioche buns.

400 g (13 oz) chicken livers, trimmed and diced
salt and pepper
½ cup plain flour
2 tablespoons crunchy peanut butter
¾ cup hot chicken stock
3 spring onions, chopped
¾ teaspoon crushed garlic
2 tablespoons olive oil
1 teaspoon ground cumin
1 tablespoon ground coriander
2–6 bird's-eye chillies, chopped
6 cherry tomatoes, halved
a handful of basil, coriander or Vietnamese mint leaves

Season the livers and dredge lightly with flour. Set aside. Mix the peanut butter into the chicken stock.

In a non-stick pan, sauté the onions and garlic in the olive oil for about a minute. Add the livers, increase the heat to medium–high, and sauté the livers until they have begun to firm up (about 1½ minutes). Add the cumin, coriander and chillies, and stir to mix. Cook for another minute, stirring, then pour in the peanut butter mixture. Bring to the boil, reduce heat and simmer for about 2 minutes, until the sauce thickens and the livers are tender. Add the tomatoes and herbs, and cook briefly. Season to taste before serving.

Serves 4

Steamed mussels with Thai flavours

Kaffir lime leaves give wondrous citrusy flavours. If the leaves aren't available, use very finely shredded lime or lemon rind, carefully scraping away all of the pith. For this dish you'll need a bowl on the table for the mussel shells, and fingerbowls of lukewarm water or tea with a few slices of fresh lime floating.

2 kg (4 lb) fresh black-lip mussels in their shells
2 spring onions, chopped
1 lemongrass stem, chopped
1 large garlic clove, sliced
1 large mild red chilli, de-seeded and chopped
1 large mild green chilli, de-seeded and chopped
4 kaffir lime leaves, or zest of 1 lime/lemon
2 sprigs of coriander (including the roots)
1 stem of basil leaves (optional)
4 slices fresh ginger, shredded
½ cup dry white wine
½ cup fish stock or water
½ teaspoon salt
a sprinkle of black peppercorns
a sprinkle of fennel seeds

If time allows, soak the mussels in cold water for a few hours to ensure there is no sandy residue within. Pull off the beards and scrape off anything extraneous clinging to the shells. Rinse in cold water.

Assemble all the ingredients and place in a large saucepan with a well-fitting lid. Set over high heat until the liquid comes to the boil, then reduce heat slightly and cook, shaking the pan occasionally but not too vigorously, until the mussels have opened (about 4 minutes). Ladle the mussels into deep bowls, picking out any that have not opened: return these to the pot, cook for another minute over a high heat, and discard any that still haven't opened. Divide the liquid from the saucepan between the bowls and serve at once.

Serves 4–6 as an entrée, or 3–4 as a main course

Seafood laksa

Using two kinds of noodles is traditional, but not obligatory. If you can't find a good marinara mix, it's simple to put together your own, using squid rings, shelled prawns and mussels, and scallops.

200 g (6½ oz) fresh hokkien noodles or 2 bundles thin egg noodles
140 g (5 oz) rice stick noodles (rice vermicelli)
400 ml (13 oz) each of coconut milk and coconut cream
2 cups water
2½–3 teaspoons Thai red curry paste
3–4 teaspoons mild curry powder
1 lemongrass stem, diagonally sliced
3 fresh or 5 dried kaffir lime leaves (optional)
1 fish (or chicken) stock cube, or 1 teaspoon Japanese dashi stock granules
250 g (8 oz) skinless white fish, chopped
500 g (1 lb) marinara mix or your own seafood selection
3 spring onions, chopped
2 cups bean sprouts
fish sauce and lemon or lime juice
salt and pepper (optional)

Follow the instructions on the pack to cook the hokkien noodles: some require cooking while others are pre-cooked and should just be rinsed in boiling water. Cook egg noodles for 3½ minutes in boiling, lightly salted water. Soak rice stick noodles in boiling water for 4–5 minutes. Drain the noodles in a colander, rinse the saucepan and return it to medium heat. Put in all the coconut milk, half the coconut cream, and the water. Bring to the boil slowly, stirring, then reduce heat to medium–low. Add the curry paste and powder, lemongrass, lime leaves, stock cube or granules, and half the chopped fish. Simmer for 5–6 minutes and then taste the sauce: the flavour should be quite strong. Add the remaining fish, the seafood and the spring onions (save some of the greens for garnish). Simmer for 5 minutes, stirring occasionally.

Divide the drained noodles and the bean sprouts evenly between 4 deep bowls. Check the sauce for seasoning, adding fish sauce, lemon or lime juice, plus salt and pepper if needed. Ladle over the noodles, garnish with the spring-onion greens, and serve.

Serves 4

Tibetan noodles with minced beef and chilli

A fabulous vegetarian dish if you use finely diced firm tofu (about 400 g or 13 oz) instead of meat. Slithery, slurpy cellophane noodles soak up hot flavours, so the amount of hot chilli paste is not as extreme as it may seem. If you want to play safe, though, reserve some of the paste to add at the end if needed.

200 g (6½ oz) eggplant, diced
salt
140 g (5 oz) cellophane noodles (bean thread vermicelli)
2 tablespoons vegetable oil or peanut oil
1 tablespoon sesame oil
500 g (1 lb) lean beef, lamb or pork, coarsely minced
1 medium onion or 5 spring onions, finely chopped
1½ teaspoons crushed garlic
1½ teaspoons crushed ginger
3 tablespoons chilli bean paste
2 tablespoons light soy sauce
1 teaspoon sugar
¼ cup water
¼ cup chopped coriander
¼ cup chopped roasted peanuts (optional)
chopped fresh red and/or green chilli

Place the eggplant in a colander and salt generously. Leave for 10 minutes, then rinse well with cold water, drain and pat dry with kitchen towels. In a large bowl soak the noodles in a generous amount of boiling water.

Heat the oils in a wok and stir-fry the eggplant for about 3 minutes, then remove to a plate. Add the meat or tofu and the chopped onion (but not the spring onions yet) to the hot wok. Stir-fry for 5 minutes (tofu will need only 1–2 minutes).

In a small bowl combine the garlic, ginger, chilli bean paste, soy and sugar. Return the eggplant to the wok and add the spring onions, if used, and the mixed seasoning ingredients, then stir-fry for 1 minute. Drain the noodles and add immediately to the wok with the water. Simmer briefly to mix everything together. Lastly add the chopped coriander, peanuts and chilli, keeping some of each to dress the finished dish.

Serves 4

Hot-sauce chicken with noodles

If you maintain a reasonably comprehensive stock of basic Asian seasonings, dishes like this are simple to produce. Purchase Chinese vegetables in small cans and keep any unused portions in fresh water (changed daily) in a covered container in the refrigerator for up to 3–4 days.

400 g (13 oz) fresh thin egg noodles
375 g (12 oz) skinless chicken breast fillet
1 teaspoon crushed garlic
2½ tablespoons hoisin sauce
1½ tablespoons light soy sauce
2 teaspoons chilli paste or chilli oil (page 142)
2 tablespoons peanut or vegetable oil
2 teaspoons sesame oil (optional)
1 large hot red chilli, de-seeded and shredded
1 large hot green chilli, de-seeded and shredded
4 spring onions, chopped
¾ cup drained straw mushrooms
½ cup drained bamboo shoots, sliced
1¼ cups chicken stock or water
3 teaspoons cornflour

Heat 2 litres of water in a wok and when it is boiling add the noodles and cook for 3 minutes. Pour into a colander to drain, and wipe out the wok.

Very thinly slice the chicken. In a small mixing bowl combine the garlic, hoisin and soy sauces, and the chilli paste or oil, mixing well. Brush 1–2 teaspoons of this mixture over the chicken.

Heat the oils in the wok over a high heat. Add the chicken, the chillies and the white parts of the spring onions, and stir-fry over high heat until the chicken is almost cooked (about 2½ minutes). Add the mushrooms, bamboo shoots, spring-onion greens, and pre-mixed sauce, and continue to stir-fry until everything is well mixed – by now you may be swooning from the heady aroma. Combine the stock or water and the cornflour, pour into the wok and stir for 30 seconds. When the sauce is somewhat thick and sticky, add the noodles and heat gently. Serve.

Serves 4

Hot doggies

Big kids' treats. I buy bratwurst from a traditional German butcher who uses plenty of seasoning and garlic. They are so meaty they hardly exude a drop of fat as they grill, so I cook them in the same pan as the onions.

1 large onion, finely sliced
1 red capsicum, cut into fine strips
1 large hot red chilli, de-seeded and shredded
2 tablespoons olive or vegetable oil
4 bratwurst sausages
4 long rolls or hotdog buns
mayonnaise, mustard, chilli sauce or butter (optional)

In a frying pan, sauté the onion, capsicum and chilli in the oil for about 8 minutes, until well cooked. If they will fit, cook the sausages at the side of the same pan; otherwise cook them separately, turning often.

Split the rolls or buns, spread with mayonnaise, mustard, chilli sauce or butter, as you choose. Divide the sautéed vegetables evenly between the buns and press a sausage on top. To serve, wrap a paper napkin around the centre of each roll.

Serves 6

Peppered mackerel on salad leaves

A salad and a creamy dressing takes bought peppered smoked mackerel onto a new plane. Smoked trout would do as well, if you add chopped chilli or plenty of cracked black pepper to the dressing.

2 x 140 g (5 oz) fillets of peppered smoked mackerel
2–3 handfuls small curly endive or small-leaved salad mix
1 tablespoon olive oil
¼ cup mayonnaise
1 teaspoon Dijon mustard

Skin the mackerel and cut it into pieces. Rinse and dry the salad leaves, moisten with olive oil, divide between two shallow bowls or plates, and arrange the fish over. Whisk the mayonnaise with the mustard, spoon over the fish, and serve.

Serves 2–3

Grilled sardines with hot honey mustard sauce

Fresh sardines are an inexpensive treat that can be cooked in a flash. If you cannot buy honey-flavoured mustard, mix Dijon mustard and clear honey to taste.

12 small fresh sardines
salt and pepper
flour
3 tablespoons mayonnaise
1 tablespoon sweet chilli sauce
2½ teaspoons honey mustard
1-2 tablespoons olive oil

Cleaning fresh sardines is easy, but messy. Put on disposable gloves and work over a double thickness of paper: use it to wrap the waste when you are finished.

Set a sardine on the worktop, stomach downwards and head pointing towards your knife. Sever the head without cutting right through, pull the sardine upwards while pressing the knife down and the gut should pull out with the head attached. Working from the underside, butterfly the beheaded sardine, cutting through the backbone but not separating the two halves. Rinse with cold water and press the sardine out flat.

When all are done, pat dry with paper towels, season with salt and pepper and coat lightly and evenly with flour. Heat a flat or ribbed iron pan.

In a small bowl combine the mayonnaise, sweet chilli sauce and honey mustard, and set aside.

Moisten the pan with the oil and when very hot put in the sardines, skin-side down, to grill until streaked with brown. Turn, and cook the other side. Do not crowd the pan: cook in two batches if necessary. The sardines will take barely a minute to cook through. Lift onto warmed serving plates, garnish and serve with a dollop of the sauce.

Serves 4

▶

A beef carpaccio with Asian flavours (page 44)

Chilli black-bean scallops

Scallops with the orange roe still attached are preferred for this strong-flavoured dish. If time and interest allow, make crunchy little edible nests for serving the scallops. Press wonton wrappers between a pair of small wire ladles and immerse in hot oil until they puff and crisp. Alternatively, fry flat until they expand, lift out while still flexible, drape over the back of a small dish and press a similar dish on top to form the shape. Leave to cool while another nest is cooking, then remove and proceed with the next.

2 spring onions, diagonally sliced
1½ tablespoons very finely diced green capsicum
1½ tablespoons very finely diced celery
2 tablespoons vegetable oil
1 large mild chilli, de-seeded and very finely diced
1 large garlic clove, finely chopped
1 teaspoon crushed ginger
2½ teaspoons salted black beans, rinsed, dried and finely chopped
24 fresh scallops
⅓ cup chicken stock
1¼ teaspoons cornflour
salt and cracked black pepper

In a wok or large frying pan, heat the oil and stir-fry the spring onions, capsicum and celery until they have barely softened (about 1½ minutes). Remove to a plate using a slotted spoon.

Reheat the pan. In the remains of the oil, stir-fry the chilli, garlic, ginger and black beans with the scallops, until the white part of the scallops is firm and opaque and the mixture is very aromatic (about 1 minute). Return the vegetables to the pan and mix well. Combine the chicken stock and cornflour, pour into the pan and stir to make a sauce that clings to the ingredients. Season with salt and pepper, and serve.

Serves 4

◄

Chilli crab (page 75)

Ceviche of quail with chilli, currants and peppercorns

In Spain, small birds are reared or trapped for the table. They are usually grilled, or prepared as a ceviche. The same method can be used for sardines or other small oily fish. Ceviche is best made the night before so that the strong flavours of the marinade have time to mellow. If you haven't planned for this, use only $\frac{1}{3}$ cup of vinegar, and add 1–2 teaspoons of sweet sherry or liqueur muscat.

4 large or 6 small quails, cleaned
salt and pepper
flour
$\frac{2}{3}$ cup olive oil
1 medium onion, cut into thin wedges, layers separated
1 large hot red chilli, de-seeded and shredded
$1\frac{1}{2}$ teaspoons crushed garlic, or 2–3 garlic cloves, thinly sliced
2 bay leaves
$\frac{1}{2}$ teaspoon black peppercorns, lightly cracked
1 teaspoon cumin seeds
$\frac{1}{2}$ cup currants
$\frac{1}{2}$ cup wine vinegar or sherry vinegar

Cut the quails in half and trim off wings and necks. Dry with paper towels, season with salt and pepper, and coat lightly and evenly with flour.

Heat half the oil in a wide pan. Add the onion and chilli, and fry for about $1\frac{1}{2}$ minutes, then remove with a slotted spoon to a glass dish or glazed pottery bowl. Place the quails in the pan, and cook over medium–high heat until golden and barely cooked through. Pour oil and quails over the onions.

Wipe out the pan and add the remaining oil and the garlic, bay leaves, cumin and peppercorns. Fry briefly, then add the currants and sauté briefly before pouring in the vinegar. Bring to the boil, stirring, then pour over the quails and turn them once or twice. Set aside until cool, then cover with plastic wrap and refrigerate.

Arrange two or three portions of quail on each plate, drizzled with some of the dressing and scattered with the currants and chillies.

Serves 4

Main Events

FIERY FLAVOURS ENLIVEN these easy main courses, most of which take no more than a few minutes to prepare. Freshness and simplicity are the keynotes, and quality ingredients will make all the difference. Be selective when you buy fresh produce: you get as good as you demand, so don't settle for second best.

This is an eclectic collection of meat, poultry and seafood dishes which take inspiration from Asia, South America, Mexico and Africa. Many are elevated on the heat scale and need moderating accompaniments. The traditional or cross-cultural accompaniments of vegetables, rice and pasta I've suggested make these dishes into complete meals, but they are intended as ideas, not prescriptions. Imaginative add-ons can transport the simple to the sublime. Indian cooks are masters at introducing cameos of flavour to their meals, with sweet chutneys tempering fiercely hot dishes, and tart pickles imparting sparkling highlights where the seasoning is less vibrant. They counter chilli burn with soothing yoghurt, and pep up grills and roasted meats with vegetables in tangy dressings. For ideas, check out the recipes in the Greens and Side-lines chapters. Invent your own salads and vegetable combinations: experiment with starch-based ingredients like couscous, burghul wheat, buckwheat (soba) noodles, and the lesser-used root vegetables such as taro and yams. Conjure up flamboyant condiments.

Tuna with pepper sesame crust

Accompany this with garlic mashed potatoes, or a salad of curly endive and cherry tomatoes in a lemony mustard mayonnaise. If the tuna pieces are on the skin, remove it by sliding a sharp knife between the skin and meat, scraping the blade of the knife along the skin.

4 thick portions tuna, each about 200 g or 6½ oz
3 teaspoons lemon juice
2½ tablespoons olive oil
1 teaspoon crushed garlic
¾ teaspoon salt
½ teaspoon chilli flakes
1 teaspoon cracked Sichuan peppercorns
1 teaspoon cracked white peppercorns
2 tablespoons chopped coriander or 1½ tablespoons chopped parsley
⅓ cup sesame seeds

Remove the skin from the tuna pieces. In a small bowl whisk together the lemon juice, 2 teaspoons of the oil, and the garlic and salt. Brush this mixture evenly over the tuna. On a plate combine the chilli flakes, peppercorns, herbs and sesame seeds. Press the tuna onto the spice mixture, covering all sides sparingly and evenly. If time allows, refrigerate for 20 minutes to set the crust.

Heat a cast-iron or non-stick pan and moisten with the remaining oil. Cook the tuna over reasonably high heat for 1½ minutes on each side, searing the surface but leaving the inside pink. If you prefer fish cooked right through, reduce the heat slightly and extend the cooking time to about 3 minutes on each side. Lift onto warmed plates to serve.

Serves 4

Tempura whiting with orange ponzu sauce

Kitchen-equipment fanciers should check out Japanese kitchenware shops for the metal tweezers used for removing bones from fish. They are inexpensive, and do double duty for capturing the odd stray feather on a chicken drumstick.

4–6 King George whiting fillets
1/4 cup plain flour

The sauce
1 tablespoon mirin (Japanese rice wine)
1 tablespoon lemon juice
2 tablespoons orange juice
1 tablespoon rice vinegar
1/4 cup light soy sauce
1 1/2–2 teaspoons finely grated orange zest
4 teaspoons wasabi powder or paste

To make the tempura
2 1/2 cups vegetable oil
1 tablespoon sesame oil
1 egg yolk
1 cup iced water
1 cup plain flour
lemon wedges

Check the whiting for bones and remove them with tweezers. Cut larger fillets diagonally into 3 pieces each. Dust lightly and evenly with flour. Before you prepare the tempura batter, make the sauce and heat the oil.

In a small saucepan heat the mirin to boiling, then remove from the heat and add the juices, vinegar, soy sauce and orange zest. Mix well and pour into 4 small bowls. Moisten wasabi powder with water and place a portion on each dinner plate.

In a wok or other pan suited to deep-frying, heat the oils to reasonably hot. When all is ready, whisk the egg and water together in a bowl, add the flour and very lightly stir it into the liquid, preferably using chopsticks or a fork. Tempura batter cooks crispest if very lightly mixed, even with a few blobs of flour left in. Dip the fish into the batter and fry in the oil for about 1 1/2 minutes, until crisp and puffy. Drain on paper towels before serving with lemon wedges and the dipping sauce.

Serves 4

Crisp-fried snapper with sweet chilli sauce

A whole fish cooked this way looks spectacular, and takes only about 12 minutes to crisp in the oil. Balance the fish on its belly on a serving plate, smother with the sauce and cover with a confetti of deep-fried basil leaves and chilli shreds. If you use fish fillets, make the dish more elaborate by serving over a mound of Asian-inspired avocado salsa (page 144).

a 1–kg (2 lb) whole snapper or 4 snapper fillets (skin on)
1 teaspoon garlic salt
¾ cup cornflour
¾ cup sweet chilli sauce
½ cup pickled shallots (optional)
leaves from 1 large bunch basil
1 large red chilli, de-seeded and sliced
2½–6 cups vegetable oil

Rinse the whole fish, check for loose scales and pat the fish dry with paper towels. Splay the lower flaps of the fish outwards so it can stand on the serving plate. Cut fillets diagonally in half. Season the whole fish or fillets with the garlic salt and coat thickly with cornflour (including the cavity of the whole fish). Set aside.

Pour the chilli sauce into a small saucepan or a microwave dish, add the pickled shallots and set aside.

Heat the oil in a wok or large pan (you will need no more than 3 cups for fillets). Meanwhile make sure the basil leaves are dry or they will splutter dangerously when frying. When the oil is very hot, put the basil and chilli into a basket and fry until crisp. Lift out the basket and set it aside over a bowl to drain.

Reheat the oil and add the fish. Fry until golden-brown, very crisp on the surface and well cooked through (about 3 minutes for fillets, 10–12 for the whole fish). Lift out and drain. To serve, stand the whole fish on its belly on a serving platter, or warm individual plates for the fillets. Quickly heat the chilli sauce on the stove, or in the microwave for about a minute on High. Pour over the whole fish or divide between plates and serve the fillets on top.

Return the frying basket to the oil and reheat the basil and chilli. Lift out, shake off any excess oil and scatter the garnish over the fish. Serve at once.

Serves 4

Seared salmon with salsa verde

Salsa verde keeps for months in the refrigerator, so I've given quantities for more than you will need for this dish. Store any leftovers in a glass jar and float a little oil on top.

4 salmon steaks
salt and pepper

Salsa verde

1 slice of heavy Italian bread, crusts removed
1 small bunch parsley, rinsed, dried well and leaf sprigs picked
1 small bunch fresh basil, rinsed, dried well and leaves picked
1 large garlic clove, peeled
½ celery stalk, or 2 spring onions, chopped
3 pickled green chillies, drained, stemmed and chopped
85 g (2½ oz) sour gherkins, chopped
¼ cup drained capers
8–10 anchovies
salt and pepper
½ cup good-quality olive oil

To cook the salmon
extra 1 tablespoon olive oil

Check the salmon for bones, season with salt and pepper, and set aside.

Soak the bread in water until thoroughly softened, then squeeze out the water and break the bread into small pieces. Place the parsley, basil and garlic in a food processor and chop finely using the pulse control. Add the bread and celery or spring onions, chop briefly and then add the chillies, gherkins, capers and anchovies. Grind to a paste, season with salt and pepper, and slowly add the oil to give a thick mayonnaise-style sauce.

To cook the salmon, first place a pan over high heat and moisten with olive oil. Sear the salmon steaks for 1 minute on each side (this leaves the inside beautifully rare, but you can cook them for longer if you prefer). Lift the fish onto warmed plates and spoon a generous amount of sauce over. Serve on a crisp oven-baked galette of thinly sliced potato, with sautéed spinach.

Serves 4

Swordfish with chilli lime butter

Most recipes for swordfish (including this one) also work for tuna, ocean trout or salmon. Sometimes I marinate thick pieces of reef fish in these citrusy flavours, too.

4 swordfish steaks, each about 185 g or 6 oz
3 tablespoons lime juice
1½ tablespoons grated lime zest
1½ tablespoons finely minced green chilli
2 tablespoons orange juice
1 tablespoon orange curaçao or tequila
1 teaspoon crushed garlic
2 tablespoons olive oil
3 tablespoons softened butter
chopped coriander or basil
salt

Check the fish for bones, and pat the steaks dry with paper towels. In a shallow dish combine 2 tablespoons of the lime juice with 1 tablespoon of the lime zest, chilli, and orange juice, and the liqueur and garlic. Whisk to mix well, add the oil and then whisk again. Place the fish in the marinade, cover with plastic wrap and leave for at least 30 minutes: you can leave it for up to 2 hours if time allows, but no longer or the acids in the citrus juice will soften the fish too much.

In a small bowl whip the remaining lime juice, zest and chilli into the butter, adding the chopped herbs with salt to taste. Shape this butter into a log, wrap it in foil and place in the freezer to firm up.

Heat a grill, hotplate or ribbed iron pan. When it is very hot, grill the swordfish steaks for about 2 minutes on each side, basting with the marinade. Before cooking further, check by inserting the point of a knife into the thickest part of the fillet: the layers of fish should separate easily.

Lift the fish onto warmed plates. Cut the butter into 8 slices, place two on each piece of fish and serve at once. This goes well with long-grain white rice cooked with coconut cream, and perhaps a stir-fry of snow peas, sliced snake beans and water chestnuts.

Serves 4

Chilli crab

Buy uncooked crabs which are absolutely fresh, preferably still alive (in which case, subdue them in the freezer for half an hour before you want to prepare them). Otherwise, buy cooked crabs from a reliable fishmonger: follow the recipe, but cook them only long enough to warm through. Set the table with crab crackers, a bowl for shells and don't forget the finger bowls!

1 large mud crab or 2–3 sand or blue swimmer crabs (total weight 1 kg or 2 lb)
flour or cornflour
2½ tablespoons vegetable oil
1 bunch spring onions, chopped, or 1 medium onion, finely sliced
1 red capsicum, de-seeded and finely shredded
6 thin slices fresh ginger, shredded, or 2 teaspoons crushed ginger
3 teaspoons sambal ulek
2½ tablespoons hoisin sauce
1½ tablespoons sugar
3 tablespoons fish sauce or light soy sauce
1 cup water mixed with 3 teaspoons cornflour

Remove the top shell of the crabs. Scrape out any inedible parts, rinse the crabs under cold water and cut into serving pieces, each with a portion of the body and a leg or two. Crack the claws, and coat all cut surfaces of the crab meat with flour or cornflour.

Heat the oil in a wok or large pan over high heat. Put in the crabs and turn them over and over, until they change colour and the floured surfaces are lightly golden. Remove to a plate. Add the spring onions and capsicum to the wok and stir-fry for about 4 minutes until cooked, then add the ginger and sambal ulek, hoisin sauce and sugar, and cook briefly, stirring. Season with the fish sauce or soy sauce.

Return the crabs to the wok and continue to stir-fry, still over high heat, until everything is well mixed and the crab shell is red. Pour in the cornflour mixture and continue to stir until the sauce clings to the crab. Check seasoning, then use tongs to arrange the crabs onto a large platter. Serve with steamed white rice and a fresh vegetable pickle (see page 79), or a sauté of water spinach or Chinese greens.

Serves 4

Prawn vindaloo

If you use a commercial vindaloo paste, this can be on the table in less than 10 minutes.

440g (14 oz) prawns, shelled and deveined
1 cup tomato juice or mixed vegetable juice
2–3 kaffir lime leaves (optional)
5–6 spring onions, chopped
1 teaspoon crushed garlic
2 tablespoons ghee, butter or vegetable oil
1–1½ tablespoons vindaloo paste
¾ cup frozen green peas, spinach or sliced beans
½ cup creamy natural yoghurt or sour cream
salt

Simmer the prawns in the tomato or vegetable juice with the lime leaves for 3 minutes. Meanwhile sauté the spring onions and garlic in a separate pan in the ghee, butter or oil until softened (about 2 minutes). Add the vindaloo paste and the vegetables, and strain on the cooking liquid from the prawns. Bring to the boil and simmer for 5–6 minutes. Add the prawns and the yoghurt or sour cream, and heat through. Check seasonings, adding salt to taste. Serve over rice, or with Indian bread and a salad of cucumber or boiled new potatoes in yoghurt with dill or coriander.

Serves 4

Clever chilli-eaters sip creamy lassi to soothe singed stomachs. This salty recipe can be pepped up with a pinch of chilli, but you may prefer it as a sweet drink made from fruit yoghurt with a drizzle of honey. For 2, you will need 200 ml (7 fl. oz) each of water and natural yoghurt, a large pinch of salt, and some ice cubes. Put everything in a blender and blend until smooth and frothy. Pour into tall glasses and garnish with a lemon or lime slice or a sprinkle of cayenne pepper.

Spicy prawn and feta casserole

At one point in my life I regularly visited Greece. This recipe was among my discoveries – I've pepped it up with red chilli.

600 g (1¼ lb) large green prawns in their shells
1 medium onion, finely sliced, or 1 bunch spring onions, finely chopped
3 tablespoons olive oil
1½ cups tomato-based pasta sauce
1–1¾ teaspoons sambal ulek or hot chilli sauce
1 teaspoon sugar
pepper and salt
200 g (6½ oz) feta, chopped
chopped herbs (parsley, coriander or basil)

Preheat the oven to 190°C (375°F). Shell the prawns, leaving the tail and last section of the shell intact. Cut deeply down the central back of each prawn and remove the dark vein. Rinse and dry the prawns.

Sauté the onions (for spring onions, use the white parts and half the greens) in the olive oil for about 3 minutes. Add the tomato sauce, sambal ulek and sugar, and mix well. Heat to boiling and check seasoning: add pepper to taste, but salt very sparingly as the feta will contribute its own salt to the dish.

Spread the prawns evenly in a shallow ovenproof dish and pour the sauce over. Cover with the feta and place in the preheated oven for about 15 minutes. Scatter with the herbs before serving in the casserole. This full-flavoured dish needs a bland accompaniment such as garlic mashed potatoes, plain white rice, polenta or just lots of crusty bread.

Serves 4

Honey chilli chicken

Fresh breadcrumbs, or chopped peanuts or walnuts, can replace the sesame seeds. Or you could use chicken with its skin on, instead of a topping: it will crisp well.

3 spring onions, finely chopped
6 skinless chicken thigh fillets
½ cup water or chicken stock
3 tablespoons clear honey
1¼ tablespoons sesame oil
4 teaspoons hot chilli sauce
1½ teaspoons salt
2 tablespoons sesame seeds

Preheat the oven to 190°C (375°F). Spread the spring onions in a casserole or microwave dish into which the chicken will fit snugly. Arrange the chicken pieces side by side on top of the onions and pour in the water or stock.

In a small bowl combine the honey, sesame oil, chilli sauce and salt (use less salt if you have made chicken stock with a stock cube) and pour evenly over the chicken. Scatter the sesame seeds over.

Cook uncovered in the preheated oven for 25 minutes, basting occasionally with the sauce. Check if done, and cook a little longer if needed. If you are using a microwave, cook on High for 8 minutes, baste with the sauce and cook for a further 6 minutes. Baste again and leave to sit for at least 5 minutes before serving. Serving suggestions: a sauté of spinach, or of sliced green and gold zucchini with shredded ginger, plus steamed white rice, potatoes just about any way, or buttered noodles.

Serves 4

Pepper chicken

When I buy chicken breast pieces, I remove the slender tenderloins and save them for satays or a stir-fry, or to cook to crisp and golden in a tempura batter.

4 chicken breasts, skin on or off, as preferred
1 teaspoon crushed garlic
1 teaspoon chilli flakes
1 teaspoon pink peppercorns, lightly crushed
1 tablespoon coriander seeds, lightly crushed
1 teaspoon ground cumin
1 teaspoon salt
1½ tablespoons finely chopped coriander leaves
2 tablespoons sesame, peanut or vegetable oil

Trim the chicken breasts of any loose fat. Butterfly the breasts by making a cut beginning where you have removed the tenderloin and working outwards on the thickest part towards the edge (but do not sever it). Fold each fillet out and you will have a large escalope of even thickness.

Combine the remaining ingredients and baste evenly over each piece of chicken. Heat a barbecue, griller or non-stick pan (preferably a ribbed one) to medium-hot and moisten lightly with oil. Put the chicken on to cook for 4–5 minutes on each side, turning carefully with tongs so you do not scrape off the crust. Rest the chicken for a few minutes before serving with fried rice or buttered pasta and a stir-fry of vegetables, or a salad. Or sandwich the chicken in burger buns with sliced red onions, shredded lettuce, tomato and sprouts, and tahini or mayonnaise.

Serves 4

 A fresh pickle of vegetable is easy to make. Simply cut your choice of vegetables (e.g. carrot, cucumber, daikon) into matchstick lengths and steep them in vinegar mixed with pink pickled ginger, sugar and salt.

Lemongrass chilli chicken

This Vietnamese dish is a classic. Peanuts contribute a delightful crunch and nutty taste: I use the large salted peanuts often packaged as 'beer nuts', as they are full of flavour. Rubbing off their skins removes excess salt, and after you have chopped them brush all of the little bits from the cutting board onto the chicken.

500 g (1 lb) chicken thigh fillets, halved
2 lemongrass stems, cut diagonally into 12 mm ($\frac{1}{2}$ in.) pieces
2 large spring onions, cut diagonally into 12 mm ($\frac{1}{2}$ in.) pieces
2 large hot red chillies, de-seeded and sliced
1 tablespoon fish sauce
1 teaspoon salt
a few twists of the pepper mill
$\frac{1}{4}$ cup plain flour
3 tablespoons peanut or other cooking oil
$\frac{1}{4}$ cup salted roasted peanuts, skinned and finely chopped

Place the chicken in a glass or stainless-steel dish. In a food processor grind to a paste half the lemongrass, spring onions and chillies, with the fish sauce, salt and pepper. Spread over the chicken, turning the pieces several times to season them evenly. If time allows, cover with plastic wrap and leave for half an hour.

The chicken cooks in about 10 minutes, so if you plan to serve it with rice you could start cooking the rice before you brown the fillets. Heat the oil to medium in a wok or heavy-based pan. Dust the chicken with flour and place in the pan with the remaining lemongrass, spring onions and chillies. Cook, turning the chicken frequently, for about 6 minutes, then reduce the heat marginally, cover tightly and cook for another 4 minutes, turning every minute. Uncover, increase the heat, scrape the bottom of the pan, add the peanuts and check the seasoning. Cook for about 45 seconds, then serve. Good accompaniments: steamed white rice, crunchy-fried shoestring potatoes or sweet potato chips, or sweet-potato mash laced with ginger.

Serves 4

Quails kai yang

Large plump quails grilled in the Thai style make an interesting main course and take just minutes to cook. Grill a few strips of bacon with the quails, dice them up and toss through a salad of mixed leaves to accompany the dish.

4–6 quails, cleaned
¼ cup fish sauce
2 tablespoons vegetable or olive oil
2 teaspoons hot chilli sauce
1 teaspoon sugar
2 teaspoons crushed coriander seeds
1 tablespoon red-wine vinegar
1 teaspoon cracked pepper
1 tablespoon chopped coriander

Cut the quails in half, rinse and drain well. Combine all the remaining ingredients in a bowl, add the quails and marinate for 20–60 minutes.

Heat a grill or barbecue to medium. Cook the quails for about 4 minutes on each side, turning several times.

Prepare the salad as described in the recipe introduction, and toss with the remaining marinade. Use tongs to pile the salad in a mound on each plate, and arrange the quail halves on top. Serve at once, with a few boiled new potatoes cut in half, and sliced asparagus cooked al dente. Or you could serve the quails Thai-style, with steamed or sticky rice and a green pawpaw salad.

Serves 4

Korean barbecue

They love chillies in Korea. If you have a pan suitable for table-top cooking, this is an entertaining way to eat with friends. A friendly butcher might be prepared to shave the meat into wafer-thin slices: if not, put the beef into the freezer for about half an hour while you get everything else ready. Partially frozen, it will be much easier to slice.

750 g–1 kg (1½–2 lb) beef steak
250 g (8 oz) fresh bean sprouts
2 medium onions, halved and very finely sliced
1 large green capsicum, cut into matchstick strips
3 tablespoons sesame oil
6 tablespoons vegetable or light olive oil
½ cup light soy sauce
2 tablespoons dark soy sauce
4 tablespoons sugar
3–4 teaspoons chilli bean paste
2 teaspoons crushed garlic
3 teaspoons crushed ginger

Cut the beef into slices as fine as you can manage, and arrange them overlapped on 4–6 plates. Divide the vegetables between the plates also, or take them to the table separately.

In a mixing bowl whisk the remaining ingredients together, and divide between small bowls for dipping. Take everything to the table and equip your guests with wooden chopsticks.

There will be considerable splattering when the food cooks, so place your table top cooker on a cloth or a large cutting board. Heat the cooker to very hot and then invite your guests to cook their own meal. First dip strips of beef into the sauce and place in the pan: they will cook in about 30 seconds. The bean sprouts, onions and capsicums can be cooked between batches of beef: stir them around as they cook so they pick up sauce from the pan. Serve plenty of steamed white rice, extra chilli sauce, and bought Chinese onion cakes.

Serves 4–6

Steaks with wasabi béarnaise

This Asian-inspired béarnaise sauce goes well with most grills. Try it with the pepper-crusted chicken on page 79.

750 g (1½ lb) eye fillet of beef, in one piece
2 cloves garlic
salt
3 teaspoons chilli oil (page 142)
1 tablespoon vegetable or olive oil

Wasabi béarnaise
1½ tablespoons rice vinegar
1 tablespoon mirin (Japanese rice wine)
1 tablespoon chopped spring-onion whites
3 egg yolks
2 tablespoons cold water
125 g (4 oz) clarified or unsalted butter, softened to room temperature
2½ teaspoons wasabi powder or paste
lemon juice (optional)

Trim the beef. Using the flat blade of a knife, mash the garlic with the salt, add 1 teaspoon of the chilli oil and rub over the beef. Cut into 4 thick steaks.

Begin the sauce before you start cooking the steaks. Simmer the vinegar, mirin and spring onion in a medium-sized stainless-steel saucepan over reasonably low heat until reduced by half. Remove from the heat and leave to cool completely while you cook the steaks.

Heat an iron pan or barbecue to hot and moisten with the remaining chilli oil and the vegetable or olive oil. Cook the steaks on the first side for at least 2 minutes before turning, then reduce the heat slightly if you prefer them medium to well done. Remove when cooked, cover loosely with foil and set aside. It will take only a few minutes to make the sauce while the cooked steaks rest.

Add the egg yolks and water to the cooled vinegar mixture and whisk over very low heat until the mixture is quite thick (about 5 minutes). Remove from the heat and whisk in the butter a little at a time. Whisk in the wasabi and salt to taste and, if needed, add a small squeeze of lemon juice. Serve a large dollop of the sauce with each steak, on warmed plates with rice or soba noodles and steamed green beans or a rocket or mizuna salad.

Serves 4

Barbecued beef and chilli wraps

Cook the steaks in a ribbed or flat cast-iron pan if you don't want to stoke up the barbecue. Make sure the pan is blistering-hot before you put in the steaks, so the surface sears instantly. That way you add plenty of flavour, while locking in all the succulent juices.

4 thick rib-eye fillets
1–2 teaspoons crushed garlic
salt and black pepper
lemon juice
vegetable or olive oil
4–8 pickled chillies, de-seeded if preferred
4 corn or burrito tortillas, or 4 pieces lavosh, lightly warmed
½–¾ cup guacamole (page 8) or mashed avocado
salsa (optional)

Butterfly the steaks to an even thickness, and bat them with a rolling pin so they are thin and quite large. Season with the garlic, salt and pepper, and a squeeze of lemon. Brush with oil.

Heat the grill, pan or barbecue. Cook the steaks to your liking. Cover each tortilla with a steak, place a pickled chilli in the centre and add a big dollop of guacamole. Season to taste, add the salsa if used, and roll up before serving. Accompany with a rice or pasta salad, or a simple green salad with tomato wedges and a vinaigrette.

Serves 4

Blackened veal

The spicy crust should be dark but must not burn. If you're cooking for offal fanciers, try liver this way: sublime!

2 veal escalopes
1½ teaspoons cracked pepper
1 tablespoon chopped parsley
½ teaspoon chilli flakes
1 teaspoon sweet paprika
2 teaspoons ground cumin
½ teaspoon dried oregano
½ teaspoon salt
2 tablespoons fine dry breadcrumbs or very fine cornmeal
¼ cup plain flour
1 large egg, beaten
3 tablespoons olive oil

The veal should be very thin so it cooks quickly. Place the escalopes, well spaced, on a piece of plastic wrap. Cover with another piece of plastic and bat each piece of veal with a meat mallet, rolling pin or other suitable weapon to spread it into a large, thin schnitzel.

In a small bowl combine the pepper, parsley, chilli, paprika, cumin, oregano, salt and breadcrumbs or cornmeal, mixing well. Spread on a plate. Dip the schnitzels into flour, coating lightly and shaking off any excess. Next dip into beaten egg, coating evenly and ensuring there are no gaps. Press the schnitzel onto the prepared crumb mixture, coating evenly. If time allows, put the schnitzels on a plate and refrigerate for at least 15 minutes to firm up the crust.

Heat the oil in a wide, non-stick or well-oiled pan over high heat. Put in the schnitzels and cook for about 30 seconds, then reduce the heat slightly and cook on the same side for about 1½ minutes. Turn, increase the heat slightly and cook the other side in the same way, first on high and then over slightly reduced heat. Carefully lift the schnitzels from the pan with tongs or an egg flip, and serve on warmed plates. Accompany with garlic mashed potatoes and salad, fried rice and sautéed beans, or a stir-fry of zucchini.

Serves 2

Veal chops with Mediterranean salsa

My little hibachi barbecue fits four meaty chops perfectly, so this is a favourite alfresco summer meal with friends.

½ teaspoon crushed garlic
1½ teaspoons chilli oil (page 142)
1 tablespoon olive oil
4 generous veal chops

Mediterranean salsa
¾ cup chopped semi-dried tomatoes
¼ cup chopped black olives
¼ cup chopped onion
¼ cup chopped parsley
1 red chilli, de-seeded and chopped
⅓ cup chopped, oil-marinated grilled eggplant
3 tablespoons extra-virgin olive oil
3–4 teaspoons wine vinegar
salt and pepper
chopped basil (optional)

While the barbecue heats, marinate the chops and prepare the salsa. Combine the garlic with the oils, and brush over the chops. Set aside. In a bowl combine the salsa ingredients, mixing thoroughly. Cover with plastic wrap and set aside.

When the barbecue is hot, brush the grid with oil and rub with a ball of paper towels to smooth the surface. Cook the chops for at least 2 minutes before turning. Like other meats that are low in fat, veal is at its best underdone so it does not dry out: cook until the surface is sealed and browned, with the inside still pink. Serve the veal on warmed plates with the salsa, and boiled new potatoes in garlic butter or fettuccine tossed with garlic and herb butter.

Serves 4

Merguez sausage sauté

African merguez sausages are potently seasoned with paprika, cumin, garlic and chilli. If you cannot get them, substitute chorizo or the most highly spiced pork sausages you can buy, and step up the heat by adding extra harissa and a sprinkle of ground cumin and paprika to the dish.

1 cup frozen peas
½ cup water
315 g (10 oz) African merguez sausages
2 tablespoons olive oil
1 large green capsicum, de-seeded and diced
1 medium-sized onion, peeled and chopped
1 celery stalk, chopped
1 large hot green chilli, de-seeded and chopped
1 large slice rindless bacon, chopped
½ cup tomato-based pasta sauce
extra ¼ cup water
1½ teaspoons harissa or other chilli paste
salt and pepper

Boil the peas in lightly salted water until tender. (Or pour them into a microwave dish, add water and cook uncovered on High for 5 minutes.)

In the meantime, cut the sausages into slices 1.5 cm (¾ in.) thick and sauté them in the oil in a wok or heavy pan until lightly browned (about 2 minutes). Remove to a plate, using a slotted spoon. Sauté the capsicum, onion, celery, chilli and bacon in the same pan for 5 minutes, stirring frequently. Return the sausages, add the drained peas, the tomato sauce and the extra water, and bring to the boil. Reduce the heat immediately, add the harissa and check the seasoning, adding salt and pepper if needed. Simmer for 2–3 minutes, then serve over couscous or sungold rice.

For a fiery pie, spread the sauté into a glass pie dish and cover with buttered filo pastry or mashed potatoes. Brush the top with beaten egg and brown under a hot grill or in a hot oven.

Serves 4

Butterfly pork steaks with gingered pears

The punchy flavours of ginger and chilli, and the sweetness of the pears, make an irresistible accompaniment to pan-cooked pork.

2 teaspoons chilli bean paste
2 butterflied pork steaks or 2 pork chops
1 tablespoon olive oil
1 ripe pear or 2 canned pear halves
2 tablespoons butter
2 tablespoons preserved ginger in syrup, or sweet ginger topping
1 tablespoon brandy
2 teaspoons flour
1/3 cup water
salt and pepper

Smear the chilli bean paste evenly over the pork. Heat a non-stick pan and add the oil. Put in the pork to cook over high heat for about 1 minute on each side, then reduce the heat slightly and cook for a further 2 minutes on each side. Remove and set aside.

Quarter the unpeeled pear and slice away the seed core, then cut each piece lengthwise in half. Add the butter to the pan and put in the pear. Cook over medium heat until the pears are tender and glazed (about 1 1/2 minutes). Add the ginger, its syrup and the brandy, and cook over high heat for about 40 seconds. Sprinkle in the flour, add the water and simmer, stirring almost constantly, to make a sauce. Season to taste, return the pork to warm in the sauce, then serve. Goes well with taro chips, or long-grain white rice tossed with roasted slivered almonds.

Serves 2

Tandoori lamb kebabs

If you cannot find dried green mango (see note below), use a tablespoon of lemon juice instead.

250 g (8 oz) lean lamb
3 teaspoons tandoori paste
1 ½ tablespoons creamy natural yoghurt
1 tablespoon vegetable oil
1 teaspoon crushed ginger

Kachumber salad
½ red onion, finely sliced
2 small ripe tomatoes, sliced
1 small cucumber, de-seeded and sliced
2 tablespoons chopped coriander or mint leaves
1 teaspoon garam masala
1 teaspoon dried green mango powder (aamchur)
1 tablespoon lemon juice
1 teaspoon sugar
½ teaspoon salt

You will need four metal or bamboo skewers. Slice the lamb thickly, cut into 3-cm (1 ½ in.) squares and thread 4 or 5 pieces onto each skewer. Beat the tandoori paste, yoghurt, oil and ginger together, and paint thickly and evenly over the lamb. The kebabs can be cooked at once, or prepared the night before, wrapped and refrigerated.

Before you begin cooking the meat, combine all the salad ingredients in a bowl and mix well. Heat a barbecue hot plate or a heavy iron pan (flat or ribbed). Put in the kebabs and cook over medium heat, turning frequently so the seasoning paste does not burn (total cooking time is about 10 minutes). Serve with the salad and Indian bread or rice.

Serves 2

Aamchur is a tart seasoning of powdered dried green mango. Readily available from Indian food shops, it gives appealing flavour highlights to vegetable dishes and salad dressings.

Racks of lamb with Sichuan pepper crust

Sichuan pepper is more aromatic than black pepper and appears less intense in flavour. But don't be deceived: it's potent enough to numb the throat if you use too much.

2 racks of lamb, each with 3–4 cutlets
1 clove garlic
1 small onion, quartered
1 teaspoon crushed ginger
1 large slice white bread, crusts removed, quartered
1 tablespoon hoisin sauce
2 teaspoons sesame oil
1 teaspoon cracked black pepper
1 teaspoon coarsely crushed Sichuan peppercorns
2 teaspoons sesame seeds

Heat the oven to 190°C (375°F). Trim the bones of the lamb rack, if necessary, and score the backs of the meat in a cross-hatch pattern to help hold the crust in place. Rest the racks on their bone ends, meat side upwards, in an oven dish.

Place the garlic, onion, ginger, bread and hoisin sauce in a food processor and grind to a paste. Press evenly over the backs of the lamb racks, smoothing the edges. Lightly brush sesame oil over the crust and coat with the peppers and sesame seeds.

Cook the lamb in the preheated oven for about 30 minutes, until rare. Remove from the oven and leave to rest for a few minutes. Separate the cutlets before serving: arrange them over a salad of small leaves, or over shredded zucchini, carrot and daikon stir-fried with a little ginger and soy sauce.

Serves 2

Mongolian sizzling lamb

If you have a cast-iron plate or pan, preheat it in the oven or on the stove, and arrange a heatproof trivet for the table so the pan can be carried directly to the table sizzling and smoky.

2 medium onions, or 1 onion and $\frac{1}{2}$ green capsicum
400 g (13 oz) lamb leg, sliced paper-thin
$1\frac{1}{2}$ teaspoons cornflour
1 teaspoon crushed garlic
2 tablespoons hoisin sauce
1 tablespoon dark soy sauce
1 tablespoon Chinese cooking wine or dry sherry
3 teaspoons chilli bean paste or 2 teaspoons sambal ulek
$1\frac{1}{2}$ teaspoons sugar
2 tablespoons vegetable oil
2 teaspoons sesame oil
$\frac{1}{2}$ cup water
2–3 teaspoons sesame seeds

Peel the onions, cut in half, then cut into very narrow wedges and separate the layers. (If using capsicum as well, remove seeds and slice flesh into thin strips.) Set aside. Toss the meat with the cornflour.

In a bowl combine the garlic, hoisin, soy sauce, wine or sherry, chilli bean paste and sugar with 1 tablespoon of the vegetable oil and 1 teaspoon of the sesame oil. Mix well and leave to marinate for at least 20 minutes.

Put the serving pan in a hot oven or on the stove to heat. Place a wok or frying pan over high heat, add the rest of the oils and put in the onions (or onion and capsicum). Cook, stirring for about $1\frac{1}{2}$ minutes, then transfer to a plate. Reheat the pan and when it is again very hot put in the lamb and its marinade. Stir-fry over high heat for about $1\frac{1}{4}$ minutes until very aromatic, moistening with water as it cooks and stirring constantly. Turn off the heat.

Spread first the sesame seeds and then the onions (or onions and capsicum) in the heated serving pan and immediately pour the meat and sauce over. Carry the pan quickly to the table while it is smoking and spluttering. Serve with plain steamed rice and broccoli stir-fried with ginger.

Serves 3–4

Cachelada

A Spanish casserole of spicy chorizo sausage, white beans and potatoes. You could substitute pre-cooked beans (about 300 g or 9½ oz) for the canned beans.

4 medium potatoes (about 750 g or 1½ lb), peeled
3 chorizo sausages (about 350 g or 11 oz), thickly sliced
1 teaspoon salt
water
a 415-g (13½ oz) can white beans or 3-bean mix, drained
3 tablespoons good olive oil
2 teaspoons crushed garlic
1 teaspoon sweet paprika
1 teaspoon chilli flakes

Cut the potatoes into 12-mm (½ in.) slices. To cook the cachelada in a conventional oven, place the potatoes in an ovenproof dish with the sausages and salt, add 1 cup water and cover with a lid or foil. Bake at 190°C (375°F) for about 30 minutes and then turn the sausages and potatoes. Add the beans, oil, garlic, paprika and chilli flakes, and cook for a further 5–10 minutes, turning once or twice more.

If using a microwave, place potatoes in a dish with the sausages and salt: add 2–3 tablespoons of water and cover with a lid or plastic wrap. Cook on High for 9 minutes, turning the potatoes and sausages once. Cook for a further 2 minutes, and turn the potatoes and sausages again, evenly distribute the beans over them and cook for a further 2 minutes on High. The potatoes should be soft, but holding their shape. Drain excess liquid from the dish. In a large pan heat the oil, add the garlic, paprika and chilli flakes, and heat for a few seconds. Add the potatoes, sausages and beans, and heat, turning and stirring carefully, until everything is combined.

Serves 4

Greens

GOOD VEGETABLES deserve pampering. They must be cooked carefully, not overdone, and never served bland and boring. Vegetables should capture attention on the plate, even beside an impressive meat. They have the advantage of bright colour and myriad tooth-pleasing textures. Vegetables and herbs are companions in the garden and the kitchen. Herbs give lively flavour and the heavenly aromas that vegetables often lack. Chilli and spices will do the same.

Legumes add substance to vegetarian cooking and allow the cook to experiment with endless combinations. Health-food shops now stock organically grown, pre-cooked beans in vacuum packs for easy use. Grains and starchy root vegetables make a plain background that cries out for added colour, shape and hyped-up, spicy, creamy and herbaceous flavours: they have impact as a side dish, but are substantial enough to enjoy on their own.

I've chosen these delicious dishes also for their versatility. Serve them in elegant portions as a first course or light snack – perhaps the Sichuan ratatouille sandwiched between feather-light crisply fried wonton sheets. Bolster a major dish with a secondary vegetable, or with rice or pasta, to make satisfying vegetarian meals: consider fiery chickpeas with South Indian potatoes, or the peppery risotto with chilli-crumbed asparagus. For non-vegetarian meals, dress up meaty mains with vegetable dishes that coordinate colours, flavours and textures: try the shrivelled beans and the gingered sweet potato with a seared fillet of beef; a big spicy grilled sausage with the corn and zucchini cakes; or prawn kebabs over Mexican rice. Keep inventing.

Fiery herb and tomato chickpeas

Ginger and dried green mango seasoning (*aamchur*: see note page 89) give this chickpea dish a vibrant flavour. A delicious vegetarian main course, it goes well with purchased Indian or Middle Eastern flatbread if you prefer bread to rice. Or serve it as a side vegetable with grilled or roast meat.

850 g (1¾ lb) canned chickpeas, or 650 g (1⅓ lb) pre-cooked chickpeas
1 large onion, finely chopped
2 teaspoons crushed ginger
1–2 large mild green chillies, de-seeded and chopped
2 very ripe roma tomatoes and 2 unripe ones, chopped
2 tablespoons vegetable oil, ghee or butter
2 teaspoons garam masala
¾ teaspoon dried green mango powder, or 1½ tablespoons lemon juice
salt to taste
2–3 tablespoons chopped coriander or parsley

Pour the chickpeas into a strainer over a bowl, then set aside the peas and the liquid. In a medium-sized saucepan sauté the onion, ginger, chillies and tomatoes in the oil, ghee or butter over medium heat for about 8 minutes, stirring frequently. Add the chickpeas, garam masala and mango powder (but not the lemon juice if used) and heat through for 1–2 minutes. Add ½–¾ cup of the reserved chickpea liquid, or water, and salt to taste. Simmer over medium heat for 4–5 minutes. Now add the lemon juice, if using, and stir in the coriander or parsley. Serve.

Leftovers can be puréed in a food processor to make a hommus-style dip.

Serves 4

▶

Corn and zucchini cakes served with a hot tomato salsa (page 97)

Corn and zucchini cakes with hot tomato salsa

Pre-soaked burghul (cracked wheat) or instant couscous would give an interesting texture to these fritters. (Use 1¼ tablespoons of dry grain for the quantities below.)

1½ cups corn kernels
1½ cups grated zucchini
½ cup finely chopped celery (optional)
1 large mild red chilli, de-seeded and chopped
2 tablespoons finely chopped onion
1 large egg
½ cup self-raising flour
salt and pepper
butter and/or oil, for frying

Tomato salsa
1 cup tomato-based pasta sauce or canned crushed tomatoes
1 tablespoon red-wine vinegar
2–3 teaspoons chopped basil or ¾ teaspoon dried mixed herbs
hot chilli sauce, to taste
1 tomato, de-seeded and chopped
1 small red onion, chopped

In a bowl combine the corn, zucchini, celery, chilli, onion and egg, and mix well. Scatter the flour, salt and pepper over the mixture and mix in well. Heat a few tablespoons of butter and/or oil in a large flat pan. Place large spoonfuls of the vegetable mixture in the pan, 3–4 at a time, and use a spatula to press them into cakes 1.5 cm (¾ in.) thick. Cook over medium heat until golden underneath (about 3½ minutes), then turn and cook the other side for about 4 minutes. Keep warm on a plate, covered with foil, while the remainder are cooked.

To make the salsa, purée the tomato sauce or crushed tomatoes in a food processor with the vinegar, basil and chilli sauce. Add the chopped tomato and onion. Warm briefly, if you like, and serve with the vegetable cakes. Good with a salad of small leaves and curly endive with black olives and asparagus.

Makes 8 medium-sized cakes or 6 large ones

◄

Racks of lamb with a peppery crust (page 90)

Spiced-up couscous

A delicious accompaniment for grilled, roasted or fried meat, or for a vegetable dish. It is also sensational as the bed for kebabs of grilled prawns or lamb.

1 cup pre-cooked or instant couscous
1 ½ cups stock or water
1 medium onion, finely chopped
1 cup grated carrot
1–2 fresh chillies, de-seeded and chopped
3 tablespoons olive oil
½ teaspoon crushed garlic
½ cup chopped parsley
½ cup sultanas or chopped dried apricots
1 ½ teaspoons ground cumin
½ teaspoon ground allspice
½– 1 teaspoon harissa or chilli powder (optional)
2 tablespoons butter
1 teaspoon salt
pepper to taste
1 ½ tablespoons grated orange zest (optional)

Bring the stock or water to the boil. Pour the couscous into a bowl, add the stock or water and then set aside for 6–8 minutes to swell and soften.

In a large pan sauté the onion, carrot and chillies in the olive oil for 2 minutes. Add the garlic, parsley, sultanas or apricots, spices and harissa. Heat through, stirring, before adding the softened couscous and the butter, salt and pepper. Stir over medium heat until thoroughly blended. Just before serving, stir in the orange zest if used.

Serves 4

Flamenco rice

I have a special saucepan for rice. It's enamelled cast-iron, with a very solid base and a tight-fitting lid, and gives me perfect results every time. Any saucepan that offers even distribution of heat, with a base thick enough to diffuse the heat up the sides of the pan, and a lid that traps steam inside the pot, will work for rice cooked by this absorption method.

2 cups long-grain white rice
2 tablespoons olive oil
1 cup tomato-based pasta sauce
1 teaspoon crushed garlic
1 teaspoon crushed red chilli
3 cups water or vegetable stock
1/2 cup green peas
1/2 cup sliced green beans or spinach
salt
6 cherry tomatoes, halved
chopped coriander and/or parsley

In a saucepan with a heavy base, lightly sauté the rice in the oil until each grain is coated. Add the tomato sauce, garlic and chilli, and cook for 1 minute, stirring. Pour in the water or stock, stir well, then cover tightly and bring quickly to the boil. Immediately reduce the heat to very low and simmer for 10 minutes. Add the peas and the beans or spinach, with salt to taste. Cover again and continue cooking until the rice is tender (about 6 more minutes). Lastly, stir in the tomatoes and chopped herbs, keeping some for garnish. Turn off the heat and leave to sit for at least 10 minutes before serving. It is good with grills, fried or roast meats, or a vegetarian main course.

Serves 6

Sichuan ratatouille

A versatile dish. Serve it as a main course with steamed white rice tossed with spring onions or coriander. Make it more substantial by adding a cup of diced soft tofu at the last minute (though you may have to boost the seasonings). Pile it on toast as a snack or entrée, toss it through noodles, or whiz it in a food processor and serve it as a dip or as a sauce over grilled or roasted vegetables or meat.

200 g (6½ oz) eggplant, sliced
200 g (6½ oz) zucchini, sliced
salt
1 medium onion, chopped
1 green chilli, de-seeded and chopped
1 red chilli, de-seeded and chopped
½ red capsicum, de-seeded and cut into 1.5-cm (¾ in.) squares
½ green capsicum, de-seeded and cut into 1.5-cm (¾ in.) squares
1 large tomato, de-seeded and chopped
2 tablespoons crushed garlic
2 tablespoons vegetable or light olive oil
1 tablespoon chilli bean paste
1 tablespoon hoisin sauce
½ teaspoon Sichuan peppercorns
fish sauce (optional)

Place the eggplant and zucchini in a dish, sprinkle generously with salt and leave for 10 minutes. Rinse well and pour into a colander to drain.

Combine all the ingredients except the fish sauce in a medium-sized heavy saucepan. Cover and cook over medium–low heat for about 25 minutes, turning occasionally. Season with fish sauce or extra salt.

Serves 2–3 as a main course, or 4 or more as a side dish

Tofu cutlets with sweet chilli sauce

In winter I serve this over stir-fried Chinese cabbage, in summer over shredded lettuce, coleslaw or small salad leaves. Steamed white rice, softened rice vermicelli, or stir-fried rice noodles with bean sprouts, all make good accompaniments too.

375 g (12 oz) firm tofu
salt and pepper
$\frac{1}{2}$ cup flour or cornflour
1 cup vegetable oil
$\frac{1}{2}$ cup sweet chilli sauce

Stir-fried cabbage (optional)
3 cups shredded wombok (Chinese cabbage)
$1\frac{1}{2}$ tablespoons oil
1 tablespoon shredded ginger
$\frac{1}{2}$ cup chicken stock or water mixed with $1\frac{1}{2}$ teaspoons cornflour
salt and pepper

Cut the tofu into 4 thick fingers, then cut each in half lengthwise. Season with salt and pepper, and coat lightly with flour or cornflour.

Heat the oil in a large flat pan. Place the tofu pieces carefully in the oil and fry until golden-brown, turning once or twice (about 2 minutes in all). Serve a portion of the stir-fried cabbage (or salad if preferred) on each plate and arrange the tofu on top. Spoon sweet chilli sauce over and serve at once.

To cook the cabbage, stir-fry in the oil in a wok or frying pan until softened (about 3 minutes). Add the ginger and the cornflour mixture, and continue to stir over medium heat until the cabbage is tender and glazed with the sauce. Season to taste with salt and pepper.

Serves 4

Grilled tofu salad with Thai dressing

You can use soft tofu, but it will need to be handled carefully so it does not break up. Cut the slices one by one, lifting them carefully into the oil on the blade of your cook's knife or Chinese cleaver.

300 g (9½ oz) firm (or soft) fresh tofu
2½ tablespoons light olive or vegetable oil
2 tablespoons fish sauce
1 tablespoon red-wine, rice or cider vinegar
2 tablespoons sugar
1 teaspoon hot chilli sauce
½ teaspoon crushed garlic
1½ tablespoons crushed roasted peanuts
100–120 g (3½–4 oz) small-leaved salad greens
60–100 g (2–3½ oz) fresh bean sprouts
½ cup loosely packed coriander sprigs
¼ cup mint leaves
1 small Lebanese cucumber, thinly sliced
2 spring onions, finely chopped, or 1 small red onion, sliced

Cut the tofu into 8 slices. Heat 1½ tablespoons of the oil in a frying pan and cook the tofu over a medium–high heat for about 1½ minutes on each side, until golden. Remove from the pan and rest on paper towels to drain.

In a small bowl whisk the fish sauce, vinegar, sugar, chilli sauce, garlic and remaining oil to make a dressing. Stir in the peanuts.

Combine the washed and dried salad leaves, bean sprouts, herbs, cucumber and spring onions or onions in a mixing bowl, with half the dressing. Pile the salad in the centre of 4 plates, and drape slices of grilled tofu over. Pour on the remaining sauce, and serve.

Serves 4

Ginger sweet potatoes

I prefer the orange-coloured sweet potatoes here, but you could use other types or yam or taro instead. Once cooked, the sweet potatoes could be puréed with butter to make a creamy mash.

500 g (1 lb) sweet potato
2 tablespoons olive oil
1 tablespoon butter
½ cup water
1 teaspoon ground ginger
⅓ teaspoon salt
1 tablespoon icing sugar

Peel the sweet potatoes and slice into 2.5-cm (1 in.) rounds. In a largish saucepan heat the olive oil and butter, and put in the sweet potato. Combine the water, ginger and salt, and pour into the pan. Cover and cook over medium heat for 5 minutes, then turn the sweet potato and cook for another 5 minutes over high heat. Reduce the heat to medium–low and continue to cook until the sweet potato is tender but not falling apart, turning once or twice. The liquid should be absorbed by this stage: sprinkle the icing sugar evenly over, increase the heat and cook for a further 1–2 minutes, turning once, until the sugar caramelises to golden-brown (be careful it doesn't burn).

Delicious with grills or a roast. Or this colourful dish makes an interesting vegetarian first course garnished with roasted crushed cashews or almonds, chopped coriander and chilli.

Serves 4

Gado gado salad with spicy peanut sauce

With time spent on arranging the components in concentric circles on a large platter, gado gado can look spectacular on a buffet table.

6–8 small new potatoes
6 corn cobettes
salted water
18 small green beans
12 snow peas (or 2 small zucchinis)
2 cups white cabbage or wombok (Chinese cabbage)
1 cup fresh bean sprouts, blanched and refreshed
lettuce leaves
2 roma tomatoes, thickly sliced
2 small red onions, finely sliced
$\frac{1}{2}$ cup small coriander sprigs

Peanut sauce
3 tablespoons smooth peanut butter
1 teaspoon Thai red curry paste
$\frac{2}{3}$ cup coconut cream (or $\frac{1}{2}$ cup milk plus 3 tablespoons coconut milk powder)
1 tablespoon kecap manis (sweet soy sauce)
salt and pepper
2 tablespoons finely chopped spring onions (optional)

Halve the potatoes and corn cobettes, and boil in salted water until tender. (Or microwave on High for 8 minutes, turning twice, until just tender.)

Cut the beans into 5-cm (2 in.) lengths, string the snow peas or thickly slice the zucchinis, and coarsely chop the cabbage. Steam until crisp-tender, or microwave on High for 3 minutes, turning once. Drain, and then combine all the cooked vegetables, including the bean sprouts. Place a lettuce leaf on each plate, pile the vegetables over and garnish with tomato, onion and coriander.

To make the sauce, simmer the peanut butter, curry paste and coconut cream in a small saucepan, stirring, until thickened. Beat lightly, then add the kecap manis and season to taste. Cool before pouring over the salad. Garnish with chopped spring onions, and serve.

Serves 6–8 as an entrée, or 4 as a light main course

A spicy gratin of cauliflower

Cauliflower cheese for chilli-lovers. Do the same with potatoes, small or sliced onions, leeks, celery hearts or sliced celeriac, or Jerusalem artichokes. I always keep crisp and crunchy dry-fried onion on hand, to add a final flourish of texture to dishes like this. It can be purchased from Asian stores and keeps for months in an airtight container.

1 small head cauliflower (about 750 g or 1½ lb)
3 tablespoons butter or a mixture of butter and olive oil
1½ teaspoons chilli powder
¾ teaspoon salt
1 teaspoon brown mustard seeds (optional)
1½ teaspoons cumin seeds
½ teaspoon cracked black pepper
2 tablespoons flour
2¼ cups milk
2 tablespoons grated parmesan
¾ cup grated cheddar
a big shake of tabasco
dry-fried onions (optional)

Rinse the cauliflower under running cold water, cut into 4 wedges and place in a steamer over simmering water. Steam for about 12 minutes, until barely cooked. Check if cooked by piercing the centre with a sharp knife: it should penetrate quite easily. If not done, cook for another minute or two.

Preheat the oven to 200°C (400°F). Using tongs, transfer the cauliflower to an oven dish and set aside, uncovered. In another saucepan, heat the butter or (butter and oil) and sauté the spices until they pop. Add the flour and stir to absorb the liquids, then add half the milk and whisk to a smooth sauce. Add the remaining milk and simmer until thickened. Stir in the cheese, and shake in tabasco to taste. Spread evenly over the cauliflower and reheat in the oven for about 8 minutes. Sprinkle with dry-fried onions before serving.

Serves 4

Malay-style water spinach

This could accompany just about anything – from a curry to a grill, from pan-fried seafood to a roast. English spinach or baby bok choy can also be cooked this way.

a large bunch (about 500 g or 1 lb) water spinach
2 tablespoons vegetable oil
¾ teaspoon dried shrimp paste (belacan), chopped
¾ teaspoon crushed garlic
¾ teaspoon chopped red chilli
1 tablespoon fish sauce, or salt to taste

Separate the spinach leaves from the stems: discard all the thicker stems and cut tender ones into 5-cm (2 in) lengths. Rinse leaves and stems thoroughly, and drain.

In a wok heat the oil to medium and stir-fry the shrimp paste for about 25 seconds, until aromatic, squashing it against the side of the pan so it breaks up. Add the spinach, garlic and chilli, and stir-fry for about 1½ minutes, until tender, splashing in the fish sauce (and a little water if necessary). Check seasoning, adding salt to taste.

Serves 4

Shrivelled beans

In China's Sichuan province, where hot and spicy tastes predominate, they have two principal seasoning styles: five flavours and seven flavours. In the former, which I've used in this recipe, chilli gives heat, garlic pungency, sugar sweetness, vinegar acidity, and salt or salt-based sauces introduce saltiness. The second style adds the bright flavour points of ginger and Sichuan pepper.

315 g (10 oz) green beans
1½ tablespoons vegetable oil
1 tablespoon water
1 teaspoon chilli paste or 1½ teaspoons chilli bean paste
1 teaspoon crushed garlic
1 tablespoon light soy sauce or fish sauce
1½ teaspoons sugar
1 teaspoon vinegar

Leave the beans whole, but trim off the stem ends. Heat the oil in a wok or pan, add the beans and stir-fry over medium heat for 1 minute. Add the water, cover, reduce heat to medium and steam-cook for 1½ minutes, shaking the pan from time to time. Lift the lid and increase the heat to high. Add the remaining ingredients and stir-fry until the beans are somewhat shrivelled and very aromatic. Serve with braised meats, grills or tofu dishes.

Serves 4

South Indian potatoes

A side dish for curries, sautés and grills. Or it can replace roasted potatoes with a baked dinner. For a vegetarian entrée or main course, serve it with a spicy salsa or chutney and a green salad. The cold leftovers can be tossed with mayonnaise, coriander (or basil) and spring onions as a salad, or sliced into a tortilla.

16 small new potatoes (about 440 g or 14 oz)
salt
1 tablespoon butter
1 tablespoon vegetable oil
1 teaspoon mustard seeds
1 teaspoon cumin seeds
1 tablespoon curry leaves
pepper

Boil the potatoes whole in lightly salted water until tender. To microwave, prick the potatoes with a fork, place in a microwave dish and add 1–2 tablespoons of water mixed with 1½ teaspoons salt. Cover and microwave on High for 9 minutes.

In a pan heat the butter with the oil and fry the mustard and cumin seeds over medium–high heat until they begin to pop. Add the curry leaves and fry briefly. Drain the cooked potatoes, add to the pan and shake around in the oil and spices until well coated. Check seasoning, adding pepper and extra salt as required.

Even when I am cooking just for myself or a couple of friends, I make up this recipe in full.

Serves 4–6

Asparagus with fried chilli crumbs

The Spanish call fried breadcrumbs *migas*, and regard them as a practical way of using up day-old bread. This simple dressing for asparagus is just as good over steamed broccoli or beans.

12 stems asparagus
2 thick slices Italian or other white bread, crusts removed
3–4 parsley sprigs
4 tablespoons olive oil
1 teaspoon chopped garlic
1 red chilli, de-seeded and chopped
salt and pepper

Steam the asparagus, or boil in lightly salted water, then drain. Meanwhile, tear the bread into chunks and chop bread and parsley to coarse crumbs in a food processor fitted with the metal blade.

Heat 3 tablespoons of the oil in a frying pan and add the crumbs, garlic and chilli. Cook over medium heat, stirring continually, until the crumbs are crisp and golden. Moisten the asparagus with the remaining oil, and season with salt and pepper. Serve with the crumbs sprinkled over.

Serves 2 as an entrée, or 3–4 as a side dish

Mexican beans

To expand this into a spicy nachos snack or entrée for 4–6 people, cook the beans and mash them. Spread corn chips in an oven dish, cover with the mashed beans, add ½ cup of a spicy salsa and cover with more corn chips. Scatter with grated cheese and bake in a hot oven or in a microwave until the cheese melts. Serve warm with sour cream and guacamole (page 8).

1 small onion, chopped
¼ green capsicum, chopped
1 small hot red chilli, chopped
½ teaspoon crushed garlic
1 tablespoon olive oil
a 750-g (1½ lb) can kidney beans or bean mix, undrained
2–3 tablespoons crumbled feta or grated cheddar
salt and pepper
¾ teaspoon hot paprika

In a small saucepan sauté the onion, capsicum, chilli and garlic in the oil until softened. Add the beans (you could use 600 g or 1¼ lb of pre-cooked beans instead of the canned ones) and cook for a few minutes, stirring frequently, until well heated. Season to taste with salt and pepper. Transfer to a serving dish and scatter the cheese and paprika over the top: the cheese will melt slightly into the beans. Serve with rice or crusty bread, or wrap in tortillas with shredded lettuce, tomato and sour cream.

Serves 2–3

Red pepper and pancetta risotto

To make this a vegetarian risotto, use vegetable stock and omit the bacon. There are no shortcuts with a real risotto, but the whole meal only takes about a leisurely half hour. Open a bottle of wine and if there is no company to share your cooking time, prop open a book: the risotto needs your time, not your full attention.

4 cups chicken stock
2 tablespoons unsalted butter
2 tablespoons extra-virgin olive oil
1 small onion, finely chopped
$1/4$ cup finely chopped pancetta or bacon
$1\frac{1}{2}$ cups risotto rice
1 cup tomato juice or canned crushed tomatoes
1 hot red chilli, de-seeded and chopped
$1/4$ cup roasted capsicum in oil, chopped
$1/4$ cup peas
2 tablespoons chopped parsley
salt and pepper
$1/4$ cup freshly grated parmesan

Heat the stock and keep it warm. In a large saucepan (a non-stick one will prevent sticking, but is not necessary), melt the butter with the oil. Sauté the onion and pancetta for about 3 minutes. Increase the heat to reasonably high, add the rice and tomato juice or tomatoes, and allow the contents to bubble furiously for a few minutes, stirring. Add the chilli, reduce the heat to medium and continue to cook, stirring occasionally, adding $1/2$ cup stock every few minutes. After about 10 minutes add the capsicum and peas, and continue until all of the liquid has been used and the rice is tender. If you run out of stock before the rice is done, add hot water; a risotto should be quite moist. Stir in the parsley, and add salt and pepper to taste. Fold in at least half of the parmesan, and serve the remainder at the table.

Serves 4

Couscous-stuffed peppers

Chorizo is a spiced Spanish-style sausage that can be found at good delicatessens. For a vegetarian dish, replace the chorizo with toasted pine nuts or chopped almonds.

3 large red or green capsicums
boiling water
1½ cups chicken or vegetable stock, or water
1 cup instant couscous
2 chorizo sausages, finely diced
3 spring onions, finely diced
1 tablespoon butter
2 tablespoons olive oil
a 415-g (13½ oz) can crushed tomatoes
1 teaspoon crushed garlic
1½ teaspoons ground cumin
½ teaspoon ground allspice
1–2 teaspoons harissa or other hot chilli paste
2 tablespoons chopped parsley or coriander, or 3 teaspoons chopped basil
salt

Preheat the oven to 200°C (400°F). Cut the capsicums in half lengthwise and use a small sharp knife to trim away the seed pod and inner ribs without piercing the flesh. Arrange the capsicum halves side by side in an oven dish, cut sides up, and half-fill with boiling water. Cook in the preheated oven for about 15 minutes, until tender. Tip out the water and leave the peppers upside down for a few minutes to drain.

Meanwhile, bring the stock or water to the boil. Pour over the couscous in a mixing bowl, and leave for a few minutes to swell.

In a large pan, sauté the sausages and spring onions in the butter and oil for 1–2 minutes. Add half the crushed tomatoes, the garlic, spices, chilli paste and herbs, and sauté for another 2 minutes. Mix into the couscous and add salt to taste.

Drain the capsicum halves and pack the couscous lightly into them, rounding off the tops. Return to the oven dish. Mix ⅓ cup hot water with the remaining tomatoes and pour into the dish, taking care not to flood the capsicums. Cover with foil and return to the oven for about 8 minutes. Remove foil and bake for a further 5 minutes, then leave to rest for a few minutes before serving.

Serves 6

Spaghetti aglio e olio

Deliciously simple. Italians from Puglia often inject little points of flavour into dishes like this by adding a crushed dried chilli. Here is an occasion for an excellent olive oil: it doesn't have to be the most expensive – save that for a salad dressing or for dipping bread into – but it should be of really good quality. And fresh garlic, please!

250 g (8 oz) spaghetti
3–4 tablespoons good olive oil
3 large cloves garlic, chopped
1 small dried chilli, crushed
freshly ground black pepper
1 tablespoon chopped parsley (optional)
2–3 tablespoons freshly grated parmesan
salt

Bring a large saucepan of well salted water to the boil. Add 2–3 teaspoons of the olive oil. When the water is bubbling briskly, put in the spaghetti, pushing it beneath the surface of the water and stirring it immediately to stop the pasta sticking together. Reduce the heat slightly when the water returns to the boil. When the pasta is done, pour it into a colander.

In a large cast-iron or non-stick pan, heat the remaining olive oil and fry the garlic and chilli over medium heat for 1 minute, stirring frequently. Increase the heat slightly, add the pasta, pepper and parsley, and toss until it is well coated with the oil and seasonings. Add a spoonful of the parmesan, and salt to taste, and toss again briefly. Serve in bowls, with the remaining cheese at the side or dusted over.

Serves 2

Spaghetti puttanesca

An easy pasta sauce. You could experiment with additional vegetable elements such as oil-marinated, roasted eggplant or capsicum, or semi-dried tomatoes.

315 g (10 oz) spaghetti
salt
olive oil
1½ teaspoons crushed garlic
1 cup crushed tomatoes or tomato-based pasta sauce
1 teaspoon dried mixed herbs
1 anchovy fillet chopped with its oil (optional)
¾ cup marinated kalamata olives
1–2 pickled chillies (or chillies from the marinated olives), chopped
2 tablespoons capers with a little of their liquid
2–3 tablespoons grated parmesan or chopped basil (optional)

Bring a large saucepan of water to the boil, salt it generously and add 1–2 teaspoons olive oil. Put in the spaghetti, pushing it under the water as it softens, and stirring to separate the strands. Cook until *al dente*, then pour into a colander to drain.

Rinse and wipe the saucepan, and add 2½ tablespoons oil. Sauté the garlic for just a few seconds, then pour in the tomato sauce, herbs and anchovy (if used). Cook over high heat until bubbling, then reduce heat and simmer for about 3 minutes. Add the olives, chillies and capers.

Add the drained pasta to the sauce, stir in half the cheese, if used, check seasoning and add salt and pepper as needed. Heat briefly, stirring and turning the pasta. Serve in pasta bowls, garnished with the remaining parmesan or chopped basil.

Serves 4 as an entrée, or 2–3 as a main course

 When you buy black olives, choose plump kalamatas and replace their brine with olive oil, dried herbs, garlic and pepper. They develop beautifully over a few weeks, and as the olives are used up the oil can go into pasta sauces or any other cooking where a distinct olive flavour will work.

Pasta shells in chilli tomato sauce

Gluten-free cornmeal pasta shells are perfect with this simple sauce.

about 3 cups cups medium-sized pasta shells
salt
1 hot red chilli, de-seeded and chopped (or 1 teaspoon chilli paste)
3 tablespoons olive oil
1½ teaspoons crushed garlic
1 tablespoon mashed anchovy fillets
a 415-g (13½ oz) can peeled tomatoes
1-2 tablespoons chopped flat-leaf parsley
freshly grated parmesan

Bring a large saucepan of water to the boil, salt it generously and add a swirl of oil. Add the pasta and cook to *al dente*.

In the meantime lightly sauté the chilli in the oil, add the garlic and anchovy, and cook for about 20 seconds, stirring. Add the tomatoes and their liquid, and mash with a fork. Cook over medium heat for 4–5 minutes, then add the pasta and parsley, and mix well. Check seasoning before serving with the parmesan.

Serves 2–4

Avocado salad with chilli lime dressing

Out of season, you could substitute snow peas (about 1¼ cups) for the asparagus.

8 slender stems asparagus, or 1¼ cups small snow peas
salt
2 ripe avocadoes
3 cups small sprigs of young curly endive
1 medium-sized red onion, cut into slim wedges
1 cup roasted red capsicum, finely sliced (or 1 cup chopped semi-dried tomatoes)
2 hard-boiled eggs or 12 boiled quail eggs
small black olives (optional)

Chilli lime dressing
1 fresh red chilli, de-seeded and finely shredded
1 garlic clove, crushed
juice of 1 lemon and 2 limes
3 tablespoons fruity olive oil
salt and black pepper
1 tablespoon chopped flat-leaf parsley
1 tablespoon chopped coriander

Slice the asparagus on the diagonal into 5-cm (2 in.) pieces, then steam, boil or microwave until crisply tender. Drain, refresh in cold water and then drain again.

Whisk the dressing ingredients to a creamy emulsion, using only half of the herbs. Cut the avocadoes in half and remove their stones, then peel the flesh and cut into chunks. Place in the dressing and turn gently to coat.

Rinse and dry the endive, separating any clumps of leaves. Divide between 4 large plates, and arrange the asparagus and onion on top. Remove the avocado from the dressing with a slotted spoon and divide between the plates, then place the sliced capsicum in the dressing and turn a few times before draping it over the avocado. Garnish with the eggs cut into wedges (leave quail eggs whole) and the black olives if used. Drizzle the remaining dressing over the salad and onto the plate. Scatter with the remaining herbs before serving.

Serves 4

Satay eggs with vegetable salad

Adding chopped nuts gives crunch to this mellow salad.

6 eggs
24 snow peas
2 cups chopped (Chinese white cabbage)
1 cup bean sprouts
2 spring onions, chopped
1 tablespoon smooth peanut butter
2 tablespoons mayonnaise
¾ teaspoon Indian curry paste
⅓ teaspoons salt
1 tablespoon sweet chilli sauce
2 tablespoons vinaigrette
1 tablespoon chopped coriander (optional)
1½ tablespoons chopped roasted cashews or peanuts (optional)

Hard-boil the eggs, then drain and place under running cold water until completely cold. In the meantime, blanch the snow peas, cabbage and bean sprouts in boiling lightly salted water, for 1 minute only. Tip into a colander and cool under running cold water, then set aside to drain thoroughly.

In a small bowl, whisk the peanut butter, mayonnaise, curry paste and salt, and in another bowl combine the sweet chilli sauce, vinaigrette and coriander, if used.

Shell the eggs and cut them diagonally in half. Scoop the yolks into the mayonnaise mixture, and use a fork to mash them into the mayonnaise until reasonably smooth. Using a teaspoon, fill this mixture into the cavities of the egg whites.

Toss the cooled vegetables and spring onions with the chilli vinaigrette, and divide between four plates. Arrange 3 pieces of egg over each, and scatter with the cashews or peanuts. Serve.

Serves 4

One-pan Wonders

FRAZZLED AFTER A DIFFICULT DAY, you need to unwind. Slip off your shoes, take a few deep breaths, and pick out a favourite CD. Spend ten focused minutes in the kitchen, then relax with a drink. Your meal will take next-to-no-time to finish. These are dishes to fit fast-paced lives: non-challenging, anti-stress home cooking that's done in minutes, in a single pan. The flavours are vibrant and revitalising. Meaty, garlicky sausages, spicy stir-fries, pleasurable rice and egg dishes, richly rewarding noodle casseroles. Quick-cook family meals and easy entertainers, they also make satisfying singles' meals with leftovers for tomorrow or the freezer.

A non-stick wok, a well-used clay casserole and a cast-iron pan that has been tended with care are invaluable kitchen assets. I also have two professional frying pans with metal handles, one just large enough for a single serve, the other of standard size. They can be put into a hot oven, and there is no better way to finish off a tortilla or a flash-seared steak or fish fillet.

Cajun prawns and okra

If you can buy very small okra, cut them in half lengthwise or even leave them whole. Cut larger okra into 1-cm (½ in.) slices.

1 medium onion, sliced
125 g (4 oz) okra, sliced
1 large green chilli, de-seeded and sliced
1½ tablespoons olive oil
220 g (7 oz) green prawns, peeled
1 teaspoon crushed garlic
1 cup tomato-based pasta sauce or crushed tomatoes
1 teaspoon dried mixed herbs
1 teaspoon ground cumin
salt and pepper

Sauté the onion, okra and chilli in the oil for 5 minutes over medium heat. Add the prawns and garlic, increase the heat a little and sauté for 2 minutes. Stir in the tomato sauce or tomatoes, and the herbs and cumin. Simmer for 1 minute, season to taste, then simmer again briefly. Serve over rice or garlic mashed potatoes.

Serves 2–3

Jambalaya

This brightly flavoured Cajun-Creole dish is as colouful as its name. You can replace chorizo with other spicy sausages, or with cubes of salami (if you do use salami, add it when the rice is half-cooked).

2 chorizo sausages (total weight about 280 g or 9 oz), thickly sliced
2 tablespoons olive oil
1 large onion, chopped
1 green capsicum, cut into small squares
1 red capsicum, cut into small squares
1 large green chilli, de-seeded and chopped
1½ cups long-grain rice
1½–2 teaspoons chilli paste, sauce or powder
1½ cups crushed tomatoes and their liquid
salt and pepper
2 cups chicken stock or water
2 cups small peeled prawns
handful of chopped parsley or coriander

In a heavy iron pan sauté the sausages for 1 minute over high heat, then remove. Add the onion, capsicums and chilli, and sauté over medium–high heat for about 5 minutes. Add the rice and stir to coat each grain with the oil, then add the chilli paste, sauce or powder, and the tomatoes. Bring rapidly to the boil, stirring. Add salt and pepper to taste, then the chicken stock, and again bring to a boil. Cover tightly and cook for 5 minutes, then add the sautéed sausages, the prawns and the herbs, and stir in. Cover and cook over medium–low heat for about 15 minutes, until the rice is done, stirring occasionally.

Check seasoning and stir the jambalaya well so that all the components are evenly mixed. Remove from the heat and leave, covered, for a few minutes. Serve in large bowls, garnished with extra herbs.

Serves 4 generously

Rice casserole with chicken, Chinese sausage and vegetables

Chinese cooks use a low-fired sand pot for casseroles like this; the pots are inexpensive to buy in Chinatown. The lightweight, buff-coloured clay pots, sometimes glazed inside, are reinforced with strong wire which makes them hardy enough to use directly over gas or in a hot oven. But avoid placing them directly on electric hotplates.

8 small dried mushrooms
1¾ cups short-grain white rice
2½ cups chicken stock
1 tablespoon chilli oil (page 142)
200 g (6½ oz) chicken breast or thigh fillet, diced
2 Chinese lap cheong sausages (or 2 bacon slices), diced
185 g (6 oz) sweet potato, cut into 12 mm (½ in.) dice
3 spring onions, chopped
4–5 thin slices fresh ginger, shredded (or 1½ teaspoons crushed ginger)
1½ tablespoons light soy sauce
1 teaspoon salt

Soak the mushrooms in 1¼ cups of boiling water for 10 minutes. Strain the liquid through a fine nylon strainer into a clay casserole or a saucepan with a heavy base. Add the rice, stock and chilli oil. Trim away the mushroom stems, cut the mushrooms in half and add to the casserole. Cover and bring to the boil over high heat, then reduce heat slightly and cook for 5 minutes.

Arrange the chicken, sausages and sweet potato over the rice in the pot. Cover and cook for about 10 minutes over low heat. Stir up the rice, add the spring onions, ginger, soy sauce and salt, and cook a further 10 minutes over very low heat. Check the sweet potato and chicken are cooked, fluff up the rice with chopsticks and taste again before serving in the casserole or a deep serving dish.

Serves 4 or more

King prawn and noodle casserole

Pepper provides the heat for this sensational Thai dish, which in Bangkok comes to the table in a clay casserole similar to the Chinese sand pot. They use giant prawns from the Gulf of Thailand, which are so big that one per person is enough.

12–18 king prawns
250 g (8 oz) cellophane noodles (mung-bean vermicelli)
2 tablespoons butter
2 slices bacon, chopped
3 spring onions, chopped
1½ teaspoons crushed ginger
1 teaspoon crushed garlic
3 teaspoons cracked black pepper
2 tablespoons oyster sauce
¼ cup dark soy sauce
2 tablespoons whisky or brandy
2–3 tablespoons chopped coriander (leaves and stems)
1¼ cups chicken stock or water
finely chopped red chilli for garnish

Shell the prawns, leaving the tails intact, and make a deep slit along the centre back of each prawn to remove the dark vein. Rinse the prawns briefly under running cold water. Soak the cellophane noodles in hot water for 2 minutes, to soften.

In a casserole that can be used on top of the stove, melt the butter and sauté the bacon and spring onions for 1 minute. Add the ginger, garlic and prawns, and sauté a further minute, turning the prawns once. Add the drained noodles, lifting the prawns on top of them. Over the prawns evenly distribute the pepper, oyster sauce, soy sauce, whisky or brandy, and most of the coriander. Pour in the stock or water, cover and simmer over medium heat for 2–3 minutes, depending on the size of the prawns. Use tongs to mix the ingredients, cook another 1–3 minutes, stir up again and remove from the heat.

Leave covered for a few minutes so the noodles absorb the sauce. Serve in the casserole, garnished with the remaining coriander and a scattering of finely chopped red chilli.

Serves 4

Tortilla Espagnole

Anything goes in a tortilla. They make great use of leftovers, particularly potato. Like quiche, tortilla can be served cold or at room temperature, with a salad. To finish it in the oven, use a large pan with an ovenproof handle, if you have one. If you don't, you can cook the tortilla on top of the stove, in which case do not spread cheese over the top.

125 g (4 oz) bacon or ham, shredded
½ red capsicum, finely shredded
1 large green chilli, de-seeded and finely shredded
1 medium green or golden zucchini, very finely sliced
1 medium onion, finely sliced
½ teaspoon crushed garlic
2 tablespoons olive oil
8 large eggs, lightly beaten
1 tablespoon chopped parsley, coriander or basil
salt and plenty of black pepper
¾ cup grated cheese (optional)

Preheat the oven to 220°C (425°F).

In the pan sauté the bacon (but not the ham), capsicum, chilli, zucchini, onion and garlic in the olive oil for about 7 minutes over medium heat, stirring frequently.

Meanwhile, in a bowl whisk the eggs with the parsley, salt, pepper and half the cheese. If you are using ham instead of bacon, add it at this point. Increase the heat under the pan to high, pour the eggs carefully over the cooked ingredients and scatter with the remaining cheese. Cook for about 40 seconds over high heat, then reduce the heat to medium–low and cook until the underside of the tortilla is golden-brown and firm (about 3 minutes).

Place the pan in the preheated oven to finish cooking. (If you are cooking the tortilla entirely on top of the stove, cook one side gently until golden and firm, then invert onto a plate and slide back into the pan, cooked side up. Continue to cook until the tortilla is firm.) The tortilla will puff up slightly: it is ready when the edges are crisp and golden, the top feels firm and slightly springy, and the cheese has melted and is gloriously golden-brown. Loosen the edges with a spatula and slide the tortilla onto a serving plate. Cut into wedges to serve.

Serves 4

Lamb biryani

Cooked in the traditional way, lamb biryani can take hours, even days, to prepare. I was delighted with the results of this expedited version using minced lamb.

1 large onion, chopped
2 tablespoons butter or vegetable oil
400 g (13 oz) minced lamb
1 teaspoon crushed garlic
3 teaspoons mild curry paste
2 teaspoons garam masala
1/2 cup canned crushed tomatoes
2 cups long-grain rice
3 cups chicken or beef stock
3/4 cup frozen peas
salt and pepper
1/3 cup roasted almonds, chopped
1/3 cup sultanas or raisins (optional)
chopped mint and red chilli

In a saucepan with a heavy base, sauté the onion in the butter or oil for 2 1/2 minutes. Add the lamb and garlic, and sauté until the meat changes colour (about 3 minutes), stirring constantly to break up any lumps. Add the curry paste, garam masala and crushed tomatoes, and stir over high heat for 30 seconds. Add the rice and stir for 1 minute, then pour in the stock and cover the pan tightly. Cook for 2 minutes without disturbing, then stir up, reduce heat to very low and cook a further 10 minutes.

Fold in the peas, add a generous quantity of salt and pepper, and cook again, tightly covered, over low heat for a final 10 minutes. When the liquid is completely absorbed and the rice dry and fluffy, remove from the heat and let stand for 6–7 minutes. Check again for seasoning, fold in the almonds, sultanas or raisins, and some chopped mint and chilli, reserving a little of each for garnish.

Serves 4 as a main course, or at least 6 as a side dish

Green fish curry

Chicken, prawns, mixed seafood, lobster or bugs all make fantastic green curries. So do vegetables of just about any kind, but particularly broccoli, cabbage and silverbeet, and white root vegetables such as turnips and daikon.

about 280 g (9 oz) firm white fish (e.g. cod, hake, Nile perch)
2 teaspoons lime or lemon juice
1 tablespoon fish sauce
1 medium onion, cut into slim wedges
1 1/2 tablespoons vegetable or light olive oil
1 teaspoon bottled crushed ginger or 2–3 teaspoons finely shredded fresh ginger
1–3 teaspoons Thai green curry paste
1 cup coconut milk
1/3 cup water or fish stock
1/4 cup sliced bamboo shoots or green beans
2 fresh or 4 dried kaffir lime leaves
salt
a pinch of sugar

Cut the fish into 2.5-cm (1 in.) cubes and season with the lime or lemon juice and the fish sauce. In a non-aluminium saucepan sauté the onion in the oil until lightly coloured (about 4 minutes). Add the ginger, curry paste and fish pieces, and sauté for 1 minute, turning the fish frequently. Add the coconut milk, water or fish stock, bamboo shoots, lime leaves, salt and sugar. Bring barely to the boil, then reduce the heat and simmer gently for about 5 minutes.

Serve with steamed jasmine rice garnished with shredded chilli, and a salad of cucumber, red onion, cherry tomatoes, pineapple, and water chestnuts or perhaps a nashi pear.

Serves 4

Creole prawns

An easy meal to throw together when you have to eat and run. If there's no time to cook rice as a side dish, soften rice vermicelli in boiling water or use instant couscous.

1 ½ tablespoons olive oil
1 ½–2 tablespoons butter
2 tablespoons chopped celery
2 tablespoons chopped green capsicum
2 tablespoons chopped red capsicum
2 tablespoons chopped onion
1 large tomato, de-seeded and chopped
1 ½–2 teaspoons sambal ulek or other chilli paste
⅓ teaspoon crushed garlic
2–3 teaspoons chopped parsley (optional)
salt, pepper and sugar to taste
140 g (5 oz) small peeled prawns
2 tablespoons dry white wine

Heat the oil and butter together in a pan and sauté the celery, capsicums and onion for 2 minutes, until partially softened. Add the tomato with the sambal ulek and garlic, and sauté for 2 minutes more. Add the parsley, salt, pepper, sugar and prawns, and cook briefly. Pour in the wine and simmer long enough for it to evaporate and the ingredients to soften properly. Check seasonings again, and serve. A tomato, corn and onion salad or salsa goes well with this.

Serves 2

▶

Moroccan chicken (page 130)

Stir-fried Sichuan squid

If you're game, sprinkle crushed Sichuan pepper over the finished dish. But warn your guests: too much can anaesthetise throats and lips.

315 g (10 oz) squid tubes or small cleaned squid
2 tablespoons vegetable oil
1 medium onion, diced
½ red capsicum, diced
½ cup diced celery
½ cup diced zucchini
1 large green chilli, de-seeded and sliced
3 teaspoons garlic chilli bean paste
1 tablespoon light soy sauce or fish sauce
½ teaspoon crushed ginger
¾ cup water mixed with 2 teaspoons cornflour
salt and sugar
crushed Sichuan peppercorns (optional)

Cut open the squid, place inside surface upwards and use a sharp knife to score it closely in a cross-hatch design. Cut the squid into 3-cm squares.

Heat the oil in a wok or large frying pan and stir-fry the onion, capsicum, celery and zucchini for about 2 minutes. Add the squid and the chilli, and stir-fry until the squid curls and becomes white (about 2 minutes). Add the bean paste, soy sauce and ginger, and stir-fry briefly. Pour in the cornflour mixture and stir over high heat until the sauces cling to the ingredients (1–2 minutes). Check seasoning and add salt to taste, a pinch of sugar and a sprinkling of Sichuan pepper (if used). Serve over rice or noodles sprinkled with more Sichuan pepper, and with Chinese green vegetables in an oyster-sauce dressing.

Serves 4 (or more if served with other Chinese main dishes)

◄

Chocolate ice-cream laced with chilli (page 150)

Moroccan chicken

Three chillies crank up the heat to the incendiary, which is how they enjoy this dish in Africa. You may prefer to play it safe and reserve one to add at the end if it's needed.

500 g (1 lb) skinless chicken thigh fillets
salt and pepper
1 large onion, chopped
3 large hot red chillies, de-seeded and chopped
2 tablespoons olive oil
1 teaspoon crushed garlic
2 teaspoons sweet paprika
2 teaspoons ground cumin
1 cinnamon stick, broken
a few bay leaves
10 pitted dates
a 415-g (13½ oz) can apricot halves in natural juice
½ cup water
1 teaspoon chicken stock powder
½ cup blanched or smoked almonds
½ cup coarsely chopped herbs (parsley, mint, coriander or basil)

Cut the chicken pieces in half and season lightly with salt and pepper. In a large saucepan sauté the onion and chillies in the olive oil for 3 minutes, stirring. Add the chicken pieces and garlic, and cook over high heat, turning so that all the surfaces of the chicken are seared. Add the paprika, cumin, cinnamon, bay leaves, dates and apricots (with their liquid), and bring to the boil. Season with salt and pepper, pour in the water and stir in the stock powder. When the sauce once again comes to the boil, reduce heat to medium–low, cover tightly and simmer for about 12 minutes. Fold in the almonds and chopped herbs, and transfer to a serving dish. Serve with buttered couscous or rice, sautéed potatoes or mashed sweet potato.

Serves 4

Kung pao chicken

In Sichuan, in the humid centre of China, they use chillies, pepper, chilli bean pastes and Chinese peppercorns together. This Sichuan dish has piercing heat.

440 g (14 oz) skinless chicken breast fillet
2 tablespoons peanut or other vegetable oil
1 medium onion, cut into slim wedges
½ cup diagonally sliced celery
½ cup diced red capsicum
1 teaspoon crushed ginger
1 red chilli, de-seeded and sliced
2 teaspoons garlic chilli bean paste or sambal belacan
2 tablespoons light soy sauce
1½ teaspoons red-wine or cider vinegar
½ cup sliced bamboo shoots, drained
½ cup chicken stock
2 teaspoons cornflour
⅓ cup salted peanuts
salt, pepper and sugar, to taste

Cut the chicken into 1.5-cm (¾ in.) cubes. Heat the oil in a wok or large pan over high heat and fry the onion, celery, capsicum, ginger and chilli for about 2 minutes. Push to the side, add the chicken and stir-fry for about 40 seconds. Add the chilli bean paste or sambal and stir-fry everything together for about 2½ minutes, until the chicken is almost cooked. Add the soy, vinegar and bamboo shoots, mix well and stir-fry briefly. Combine the stock and cornflour, add to the pan and cook over high heat to thicken the sauce. Stir in the peanuts and season to taste with salt, pepper and sugar. Serve over rice or rice noodles with a stir-fry of Chinese cabbage, snow peas or green beans.

Serves 4

Green curry of duck

A sizzler! If you have access to a Chinese barbecue shop, buy half a roast duck for this recipe. Otherwise, buy a fresh or frozen duck and use just the breasts. The remainder makes an elegant Asian-inspired soup: simmer it in water with shiitake mushrooms, cubes of daikon or choko, spring onions, star anise and ginger.

½ Chinese-style roasted duck or 2 large duck breast fillets
3 teaspoons Thai green curry paste
400 ml (13 fl. oz) coconut cream
¾ cup water
100 g green or snake beans, cut into 5-cm (2 in.) lengths
1 medium zucchini, sliced
half a 415-g (13½ oz) can small straw mushrooms or champignons, drained
3 fresh or 5 dried kaffir lime leaves (optional)
1½ tablespoons fish sauce
3 teaspoons sugar
6 sprigs fresh green peppercorns, or 1 tablespoon green peppercorns in brine
2–3 teaspoons lime juice (optional)
a handful of fresh basil leaves (optional)

Bone the roasted duck and cut the meat into bite-sized chunks. If using fresh duck breasts, score the skin and season lightly with salt and pepper: place in a very hot saucepan lightly moistened with vegetable oil, sear the surfaces, then reduce the heat to medium and cook for about 6 minutes, till rare. Use tongs to lift the duck onto a plate, then cover loosely with foil and leave to stand.

In the pan used for the duck breasts, heat the curry paste for about 30 seconds, then add two-thirds of the coconut cream and bring barely to the boil. Reduce heat and simmer for about 2 minutes. Add the water and the beans, and simmer for another 2 minutes. Add the zucchini, mushrooms, lime leaves, fish sauce and sugar, and simmer for about 5 minutes, until the vegetables are cooked. Add the remaining coconut cream, the peppercorns and lime juice, and the basil leaves if used. Reduce heat and put the chunks of roasted duck or the thinly sliced duck breasts into the sauce to gently warm through (do not allow to boil). Transfer to a serving dish and serve with steamed white rice or coconut rice. Or add rice noodles and bean sprouts and serve laksa-style, in deep bowls.

Serves 4

Sichuan stir-fry of beef

A fast and flavoursome way to expand a single steak into a meal for two. If bottled Sichuan sauce is not available, use 1½ teaspoons of sambal ulek and 2½ teaspoons of hoisin sauce.

200 g (6½ oz) rump steak
1 tablespoon Sichuan sauce
1 tablespoon light soy sauce
2 tablespoons vegetable oil
3 spring onions, chopped
1 red chilli, de-seeded and sliced
⅓ cup sliced bamboo shoots
12 snow peas or 4 stems asparagus, sliced diagonally
½ cup chicken stock or water
1½ teaspoons cornflour
crushed Sichuan pepper
sugar

For the beef to be tender, it must be cut into paper-thin slices. Use your sharpest knife, or ask a trusted butcher to slice the meat for you. Place the slices in a bowl with the Sichuan sauce and soy sauce, and leave for 10 minutes.

Heat the oil in a wok and stir-fry the beef over very high heat for about a minute, then remove to a plate. Add the spring onions, chilli, bamboo shoots and snow peas or asparagus, and stir-fry for about 1½ minutes. Combine the chicken stock or water with the cornflour, and stir into the sauce. Continue to stir over high heat until the sauce begins to thicken (about 40 seconds). Return the meat to the pan and check the seasoning, adding pepper and a pinch of sugar if needed.

Serve over white rice with a garnish of coriander sprigs, or over a cake of fried egg noodles.

Serves 2

Creole liver sauté

As a variation on this theme, substitute 2 teaspoons of grated orange zest for the tomatoes and add a squeeze of orange juice with the vinegar.

200 g (6½ oz) calf's or lamb's liver
salt and pepper
flour
½ cup olive oil
1 small onion, cut into thin wedges
1 teaspoon crushed garlic
2 tomatoes, de-seeded and chopped
⅓ teaspoon dried thyme
½ teaspoon chilli flakes or 1 teaspoon chopped red chilli
1½ tablespoons red-wine vinegar
½ cup water
2 tablespoons chopped parsley

Slice the liver reasonably thin, trimming away sinews and skin, then cut into small escalopes. Season with salt and pepper, and coat lightly with flour. Heat the oil in a large frying pan and sear the liver for about a minute, turning each piece twice. Remove to a plate.

Reheat the pan, add the onion and sauté for 1 minute. Add the garlic, tomatoes, thyme and chilli, and cook over high heat, stirring almost continually, until the tomatoes soften (about 2 minutes). Sprinkle in the vinegar and allow it to evaporate, then return the liver to the pan and cook for about 40 seconds. Add the water and the parsley, and simmer, stirring, to make a sauce. Check seasoning, adding salt and pepper to taste.

This is delicious with crisply fried or toasted croutes of bread, or garlic mashed potatoes.

Serves 2

Ma po dofu

Fresh soft tofu (beancurd) gives this dynamic dish from China's Sichuan province a seductive, velvety texture that belies its volatile chilli-and-pepper heat.

350 g (11 oz) minced beef
1½ teaspoons crushed garlic
5 spring onions, chopped
2 tablespoons oil
1–1¼ tablespoons chilli bean paste or Thai chilli paste (nam prik phao)
1 tablespoon Chinese cooking wine or dry sherry
1½ tablespoons dark soy
1 teaspoon sugar
1¼ cups water
350 g (11 oz) soft tofu, cut into cubes
⅓ cup sliced straw mushrooms, or ½ cup chopped oyster mushrooms
2 teaspoons cornflour mixed into ¼ cup water
salt
½–1 teaspoon crushed Sichuan peppercorns
1 teaspoon crushed ginger
coriander sprigs (optional)

In a wok or large pan brown the beef, garlic and the white parts of the spring onions in the oil for 3 minutes. Stir in the chilli paste, wine, soy sauce and sugar, and cook for 1 minute, stirring briskly. Add the water, bring to the boil and simmer for 2–3 minutes. Add the tofu and mushrooms, and half the onion greens.

Pour the cornflour mixture into the pan and stir carefully (so you don't crush the tofu) until the sauce thickens. Check seasoning, adding salt to taste, plus the Sichuan pepper and ginger. Garnish with the remaining onion greens, or with sprigs of coriander if preferred. Serve with plain steamed rice or over softened cellophane noodles.

Serves 4

Pork and peppers stir-fry

This looks sensational if you use red, yellow, green and black capsicums and chillies. Serve it with steamed white rice and sautéed water spinach, or fried rice.

250 g (8 oz) lean pork (e.g. a butterflied pork steak)
1½ tablespoons vegetable oil
2 teaspoons sesame oil (optional)
1½ cups capsicum, cut into julienne
1–2 tablespoons fresh chilli, de-seeded and finely shredded
2 large spring onions, cut into 5-cm (2 in.) lengths and shredded
3–4 slices fresh ginger, finely shredded
100 g (3½ oz) bean sprouts, rinsed and drained
2 tablespoons teriyaki marinade
2½ teaspoons cornflour
¾ cup chicken stock or water
salt and pepper

Slice the pork very thinly, then cut into matchstick shreds. In a wok or large pan, heat the vegetable oil over a high flame. Add the sesame oil and the pork, and stir-fry for 30 seconds. Add the capsicum, chilli, spring onions and ginger, and stir-fry for about 3 minutes until the capsicum has wilted. Add the well-drained bean sprouts and the teriyaki marinade, and stir-fry over high heat for 30 seconds.

Mix the cornflour into the stock or water, pour into the pan and stir until the sauce thickens and clings to the ingredients. Check seasoning, adding salt and pepper to taste.

Serves 4

Side-lines

THIS CHAPTER EXTENDS the tongue-tingling experience into quick and easy home-made condiments. Stock up, keeping them in airtight containers or in the refrigerator or freezer.

Chillies, pepper, mustard and Chinese peppercorns sparkle in this versatile collection: with these recipes on hand, you have endless opportunities to brighten simple dishes. There are dressings for salads and hot or cold cooked vegetables. There are seasoned oils for dipping and for dunking and for swirling into bright flourishes of colour on large white plates. There is an international assembly of salsas to embellish grills and fries, or perhaps to serve as dips with corn chips and whipped yoghurt or sour cream. There are flavoured butters for offering in small pots with warmed loaves, for spreading on crackers, for stuffing fried chicken, Kiev-style, or for melting over grilled meats and seafood. And there are fragrant, spiced salts and peppers to sprinkle on grills, into marinades and dressings, and to serve in small dishes in the Asian style for dipping crisp-fried pastries and meats. Use these taste-packed asides lavishly with mildly seasoned dishes and selectively with other fiery dishes.

Salad dressings

Sweet chilli mayo
Stir 1½ tablespoons of sweet chilli sauce and 2 teaspoons of chopped coriander, basil or mint into 4 tablespoons of mayonnaise. Pep it up further, if you like, with a teaspoon of hot chilli sauce.

Curry mayo
Beat 1 teaspoon of Thai red curry paste or 2 teaspoons of mild curry powder into 3 tablespoons of your favourite mayonnaise. Add a big squeeze of fresh lime or lemon juice.

Satay-flavoured mayo
Beat 1 tablespoon of bottled satay sauce and 2 tablespoons of sour cream into 3 tablespoons of well-flavoured mayonnaise.

Chilli and chive vinaigrette
Add 1 teaspoon each of minced green chilli and chopped chives to a vinaigrette (1 tablespoon vinegar, 3 tablespoons olive oil) and season with salt and a pinch of sugar.

Jalapeno vinaigrette
Very finely chop 1 canned jalapeno chilli (or 2 bottled green chillies). Combine 1 teaspoon of the preserving liquid, 1½ tablespoons white-wine vinegar and ½ cup vegetable or peanut oil. Whisk this mixture with 1 teaspoon of sugar, a little salt and pepper, the chopped chilli and 1 crushed garlic clove. This mix will keep for several weeks: serve as it is, or measure out what you need and add 1–2 teaspoons finely chopped chives.

Spice mixes

Spiced salts are great sprinkled over hot chips or potato wedges or (in the Chinese way) used as a dip for grills and fried foods. Allow the mix to cool before use. Spicy peppers are an easy way to add bright flavours to grills, noodles and rice, salad dressings, gratin toppings or plain steamed vegetables.

Chilli salt

Heat 2 tablespoons of fine table salt for 1 minute in a dry pan over medium heat. Add 1 teaspoon of mild red chilli powder and 1 teaspoon of ground white pepper. Remove the pan from the heat and swirl the salt around to mix it with the peppers. For a fiery Chinese version, replace the chilli powder and white pepper with finely ground Sichuan peppercorns.

Five-spice salt

Heat 1½ tablespoons of fine salt for 1 minute, then add 1 teaspoon of five-spice powder.

Caribbean lime pepper

Place a few strips of lime and lemon zest on a paper towel in the microwave and microwave until dry (about 3 minutes). Or dry in a low oven for about 8 hours. Grind in a spice grinder to a coarse powder, then measure: for every 2 teaspoons of powdered peel, add 1 teaspoon each of salt and ground pepper and grind briefly. Store in an airtight container.

Lemon pepper

Prepare as above, using only lemon zest and half the quantity of salt.

Japanese pepper

Combine 1 teaspoon each of ground Sichuan pepper, chilli flakes, very finely chopped nori seaweed and white sesame seeds. The mixture must be kept dry to maintain its flavour.

Oils, dunks and spreads

Chewy Italian, Turkish, sourdough or pita breads are boring just with butter and traditional spreads. They need seasoned oils and peppy dunks. Most of these will keep for weeks in the fridge: bring oils to room temperature before use.

Chilli oil

For dipping, serve in small shallow dishes or saucers. But don't keep this just for bread: shake it into stir-fries, salad dressings and sauces, or over seafood or grills.

Place 5–6 de-seeded red chillies in a food processor with 1 cup of oil. Process using the pulse control, then transfer to a small saucepan. Boil for 2 minutes, leave to cool, then strain. It is now ready to use or to store.

For a peppered version, add 2 cloves garlic and 1 teaspoon of black peppercorns to the mixture in the saucepan. Then continue as above.

Hot sesame oil

In a screwtop jar combine ¼ cup of sesame oil, ¼ cup peanut or vegetable oil and 2 tablespoons of chilli flakes. Shake well and then set aside in a cool place for at least 10 days, shaking the jar occasionally. You can strain out the chillies, or leave them in the oil. In a cool corner of the pantry (or, better still, the fridge) this oil will keep for many months.

Coriander pesto oil

For a dip with bread, use the bright-green oil from the surface of the pesto. You can top up the oil as needed: always allow a few hours for the flavours to develop. The pesto itself can be retrieved from the jar with a slotted spoon for use on noodles and salads, and as a spread.

In a food processor put 1 medium-sized bunch of coriander, chopped; and 2 large dark green chillies, de-seeded and chopped. Add 2 tablespoons of roasted blanched almonds (or 3 tablespoons of ground almonds) and a teaspoon of salt. Chop finely, then slowly add ½ cup of light vegetable or peanut oil. Process to an oily paste, then add the remaining oil and purée briefly. Transfer to a glass container and allow the pesto to stand for at least 3 hours before using. For longer storage, cover with a film of oil.

Hot and spicy dukkah

Nutty, spicy dips like this originate in the Middle East. To use, dip bread into good olive oil or a flavoured oil, then press into the dukkah.

In a small frying pan or saucepan without oil, toast 2 tablespoons of sesame seeds, 2 tablespoons of sunflower seeds, 2 teaspoons of coriander seeds and 1 teaspoon of cumin seeds for about 2 minutes, shaking the pan frequently. Pour the toasted seeds into a food processor fitted with the metal blade, or a spice/coffee grinder: grind to the consistency of coarse breadcrumbs, then transfer to a microwave dish. Next grind 1/4 cup of smoked almonds with 1 teaspoon of granulated or powdered garlic, 1/2 teaspoon of salt and 1 1/2 teaspoons of chilli flakes. Add to the ground seeds and microwave on High for 1 1/2 minutes. Leave to cool completely before storing in an airtight jar.

Red pepper jam

You can spread this fiery jam on bread, or serve it as a condiment for grills and roast meat.

In a small non-aluminium saucepan combine 1 cup of finely chopped grilled red capsicums in oil, 1 teaspoon of crushed garlic, 2 teaspoons of sambul ulek and 1 tablespoon of sugar. Cook over medium heat until the mixture is thick and pasty, adding salt and pepper to taste. If you prefer a little extra sweetness, add 1 tablespoon of currants and cook until they soften. When cool, store the jam in a sterilised container in the refrigerator. Keep a film of vegetable oil on the surface of the jam to help prevent mould growth and keep the flavour and colour fresh.

Mamba

My friend Jessica B. Harris, author of a fascinating book on Caribbean cooking entitled *Sky Juice and Flying Fish*, introduced me to this fiery Jamaican-style peanut butter, which is a sensation on toast. Conveniently pre-spiced, it's ideal for satay or other peanut sauces, or you can stir a spoonful into your favourite curry for extra piquancy and creaminess.

In a food processor fitted with the metal blade combine 1 1/2 cups of skinned, salted roasted peanuts, 2 teaspoons of peanut oil and 1 teaspoon of sambal ulek. Grind to the desired crunchiness, then check for salt, adding some if needed. You may also want to add a little more oil if the paste seems dry. Store in a covered jar.

Coriander garlic dipping oil

A tasty dip for boiled shellfish or grilled chicken, this is best made at least 20 minutes before you need it.

Finely chop 2 tablespoons of coriander stems and leaves. Add 1/2 teaspoon of salt, 1/2–1 teaspoon of chilli flakes, 1 teaspoon of crushed garlic and about 1–2 tablespoons of oil.

Sassy sauces

Vietnamese dipping sauce

Mix together the juice of 1 lime, 2 teaspoons of palm sugar or white sugar, 2¼ tablespoons of fish sauce, 1 small red chilli, very finely chopped, and 1 tablespoon water

Chilli-spiked pesto

Sensational tossed through pasta, spread on toasted focaccia, or as a sauce or side dish to liven up a simple grill.

In a food processor chop the leaves of 1 bunch of basil with 1 large red chilli, 1 large garlic clove, ½ teaspoon of salt and 1 tablespoon of pine nuts. When very pasty, add ⅓ cup of olive oil and 1–2 tablespoons of grated parmesan.

Salsas

The Mexicans were onto a good thing when they invented salsa: fruity, crunchy, herbaceous, spicy – there are heaps of options for mix-and-match ingredients and flavours. Salsas are great with fried things, grills and barbecues, and with roast meats. And why not partner them with bought meats such as patés, terrines and meatloaf, or cha siew and roast duck from a Chinatown barbecue shop. For all the following recipes, combine the ingredients in quantities to suit your own taste.

- *tropical salsa* Finely diced pawpaw, diced red onion and diced (unpeeled) continental cucumber, chopped coriander. Season with lime juice, salt and pepper, chopped fresh or pickled red chilli, and chopped chives.
- *Mexican salsa* Chopped, de-seeded ripe red tomato, chopped green (unripe) tomato, chopped green capsicum and chopped jalapeno chilli. Season with vinegar, salt, pepper, sugar and chopped coriander or mint.
- *Yucatan salsa* Corn kernels, chopped red capsicum, chopped onion, finely chopped green chilli or Jalapeno chillies. Season with salt, pepper and sugar. Delicious filled into avacado halves.
- *Singapore salsa* Chopped water chestnuts or bangkuang (yam bean), chopped garlic chives, chopped red chilli and/or capsicum, chopped continental cucumber (unpeeled, but seeds removed) and chopped blanched green beans. Season with pink pickled ginger, sesame oil, salt, sugar and chilli oil.
- *avocado salsa* Combine 2 diced avocadoes, 2 de-seeded and diced roma tomatoes, 1 chopped medium-sized red onion and 1½ tablespoons chopped pink pickled ginger. Whisk together 2 tablespoons lime juice and 1 tablespoon fish sauce with sugar, salt and pepper to taste, and add 1–2 tablespoons of chopped coriander or chives.

Flavoured butters

Pepped-up butters for grilled meats and fish, for jacket potatoes – the possibilities are endless. First soften butter to room temperature, or use margarine or spreadable butter. Then make any of the following combinations, adjusting the quantities to your taste. Pop the mixture back into the fridge for a few minutes to firm up, or form into a sausage shape on foil, roll up and chill until firm enough to slice. Flavoured butters can be frozen.

- 1 teaspoon cayenne pepper or chilli powder to $1/3$ cup butter
- 1 teaspoon crushed green peppercorns and $1 1/2$ teaspoons chopped coriander to $1/2$ cup butter
- 1 tablespoon minced black olives to $1/2$ cup butter
- $1 1/2$ teaspoons Thai red curry paste to $1/3$ cup butter
- $1 1/2$ teaspoons crushed garlic, $1/3$ teaspoon cracked pepper and 2 teaspoons minced herbs to $1/2$ cup butter
- $1 1/2$ teaspoons chilli paste or sambal ulek to $1/3$ cup butter
- 1 teaspoon cumin seeds to 3 tablespoons butter
- 1 teaspoon garam masala to 3 tablespoons butter
- $1/3$ teaspoon turmeric and 2 teaspoons finely chopped red chilli to $1/3$ cup butter
- 2 teaspoons lemon or lime zest and 3 teaspoons sweet chilli sauce to $1/3$ cup butter

Fiery Finales

THESE SWEETS CHALLENGE the notion that desserts cannot be hot or spicy. The Mexicans discovered the natural synergy of chocolate and chilli tens of centuries ago. Their pungent savoury *mole* sauces are thickened and enriched with discs of sugary Mexican chocolate, and they have a sensational national recipe for chocolate cookies spiked with chilli. The French masters consider green peppercorns de rigueur in a *coulis de fraises*, just as they enjoy a dusting of black pepper or a splash of balsamic vinegar over plump fresh strawberries. Ginger has long been a classic flavouring for sweet dishes of many kinds.

So the notion of spicing ice-creams, tarts and puddings with pepper and chilli is not new. But it is exciting. Green chillies and fresh peppercorns have a clean, fresh flavour that is particularly advantageous in light fresh and fruity applications such as the peppercorn sorbet in this chapter. Black pepper and ground ginger both impart layerings of flavour that range from the subtle through to the strident. Red chillies have an affinity with creamy, sweet and sugary fruits such as bananas, apricots and pears. But they are particularly effective with dried fruits, where their heat highlights in combination with spices like cinnamon, cardamom and cloves produce exceptional nuances of flavour.

Try these heat-spiked desserts. If you don't yet dare, but still want a fiery finale to a meal, serve candied or choc-coated chillies with coffee, or slip a de-seeded red chilli and a handful of cardamom seeds into the coffee pot.

Five-minute chocolate ginger pie

A versatile recipe. As well as making a rich filling for a pie, torte or flan, it is thick enough to sandwich in a split vanilla or chocolate cake, or to layer with puff pastry as a slice. And it makes a decadent chocolate sauce: just use less cornflour.

a 23-cm (9 in.) pre-baked shortcrust pie shell or flan base
1 cup unsweetened cocoa
2 teaspoons ground ginger
$\frac{1}{2}$ cup fine white sugar
3 tablespoons cornflour (1$\frac{1}{2}$–2 tablespoons for a sauce)
2 cups milk
$\frac{1}{2}$ cup chocolate chips (optional)
whipped cream or sour cream, for serving
ginger syrup (optional)

If you have an unbaked pie shell, line it with foil, put in a layer of rice and place (frozen) in the oven to cook at 200°C (400°F) for about 10 minutes. Then remove the foil and rice, and cook for another few minutes until lightly golden.

Combine the cocoa, ginger, sugar and cornflour in a medium-sized saucepan and add half the milk. (If you are making a sauce, only use 1$\frac{1}{2}$–2 tablespoons of cornflour.) Heat gently, whisking to incorporate the dry ingredients, and when well mixed add the remaining milk. Cook over low heat, stirring continually, until very thick and smooth. Fold in the chocolate chips and spread into the pie crust, then refrigerate to chill and firm.

To microwave, combine the cocoa, ginger, sugar and cornflour in a microwave dish large enough to also hold the milk. (Again, if you are making a sauce, only use 1$\frac{1}{2}$–2 tablespoons of cornflour.) Add $\frac{1}{2}$–$\frac{3}{4}$ cup of the milk and stir until everything is well blended and smooth, then slowly whisk in the remaining milk. Microwave on High for 3 minutes, then open the oven and whisk the mixture. Microwave for a further minute and whisk again, then microwave for 1 minute more, still on High. Remove from the oven, whisk smooth, then fold in the chocolate chips and spread the filling immediately into the pie crust.

Serve the pie cold, with the cream and some ginger syrup.

Serves 6–8

Chocolate chilli ice-cream

Chilli and black pepper give a stimulating finish to this decadently rich ice-cream. I find that purchased honey biscuits or a praline of chopped walnuts go well with it.

2 cups milk
1 cup unsweetened cocoa
¾ cup sugar
4 fresh or dried bird's-eye chillies
1 egg, lightly beaten
1 teaspoon hot chilli sauce
1 teaspoon finely ground black pepper
300 ml (10 fl. oz) cream

Combine the milk, cocoa, sugar and chillies in a small non-aluminium saucepan and bring to the boil, stirring. Simmer for 3–4 minutes, then remove from the heat and leave to stand for 15 minutes until cooled to room temperature. Remove the chillies.

Chill an ice-cream maker, or rinse a stainless-steel dish.

Using a whisk or electric beater beat the egg, chilli sauce, pepper and cream into the chocolate mixture. Pour into the bowl of an ice-cream maker and churn for 25–30 minutes. Transfer to a freezer container, cover with foil, and freeze. If you don't have an ice-cream machine, pour the mixture into the stainless-steel dish, cover and freeze for about 1½ hours. Break up and beat with an electric beater until smooth, then re-freeze.

Note: a tablespoon or two of glucose beaten into the mixture gives any home-made ice-cream extra smoothness.

Serves 6–8

Green peppercorn sorbet

When my regular fruit and vegetable supplier has fresh green peppercorns in stock, I can use up a punnet in no time. I pickle some in brine, toss whole sprigs into a Thai 'jungle' curry with wild and cultivated mushrooms and game meat, and I make up a batch of this tangy sorbet to serve with sweet tropical fruits.

300 g (9½ oz) fine white sugar
550 ml (about ¾ pt) water
50 ml (1½ fl. oz) lime or lemon juice
50 g (1½ oz) fresh green peppercorns (or peppercorns in brine, well rinsed)
2 teaspoons finely grated lime or lemon zest
a small pinch of salt (omit if using peppercorns in brine)
1 egg white, lightly whisked

Bring the sugar and water to the boil with half the lime juice, the peppercorns, lime zest and salt (if used), and simmer gently for 8–10 minutes. Remove the resulting syrup from the heat and leave to cool completely.

Pour syrup through a strainer and transfer the contents of the strainer to a blender with ¾ cup of the syrup. Process to break up the peppercorns, then pour into an ice-cream maker with the remainder of the syrup and citrus juice. Churn for about 15 minutes, add the egg white and continue to churn until white and thick. Transfer to a freezer container, cover with foil and freeze until needed.

If you do not have an ice-cream maker, freeze the mixture (without adding the egg white) in a stainless-steel mixing bowl for about 1¼ hours. Break up with a fork and whip to a soft fluff with a hand-held electric mixer, blending in the egg white, then return to the freezer. Repeat this procedure when the sorbet has frozen again, then transfer to a freezer container, cover with foil and freeze until needed.

Serves 6–8

Fruity flambé

Lavish this over ice-cream, wrap it in buttered filo, or serve it with thick cream over crêpes, pancakes or sliced panettone. The fruit can be cooked ahead of time and gently warmed before flaming.

a 425-g (13½ oz) can apricot halves in natural juice
1 cup dried figs, quartered
½ cup raisins
1 cup pitted prunes
¼ cup brown sugar
1 cinnamon stick
1 teaspoon black peppercorns
4 cloves
3 bay leaves
2 tablespoons butter
2 tablespoons brandy, whisky or rum

In a non-aluminium saucepan, combine the apricots and their juice with the dried fruits, sugar, spices and bay leaves. Bring to the boil, reduce heat and simmer covered for 10 minutes, then uncover and continue to simmer until the mixture is thick and the fruit collapsing (about 10 more minutes).

To serve, melt the butter in a non-stick pan (preferably not cast-iron, as it may affect the flavour of the fruit). Add the fruit, heat through, then pour the liquor over and ignite with a match. Allow to flame, gently agitating the pan. When the flame dies down, stir the fruit and serve at once.

Serves 12

Chilli-poached pears

Choose pears that are ripe but still firm. You could, alternatively, use peeled and quartered quinces, nashi pears or small eating apples.

150 g (5½ oz) light palm sugar or light brown sugar
½ cup water
6 pears
½ cup semi-sweet white wine
½ cup orange juice
3 thin slices fresh ginger
1 small hot red chilli, de-seeded and chopped
1 small cinnamon stick
2 cloves
1 star anise

In a non-aluminium saucepan that will comfortably fit the pears, boil the sugar and water gently to make a light caramel (about 8 minutes). Meanwhile, peel the pears, leaving them whole with stems intact.

Add the remaining ingredients to the caramel and simmer briefly, then stand the pears in the liquid and cover tightly. Cook without disturbing for about 8 minutes, then baste with the liquid and cook for a further 5–6 minutes over a medium heat. Baste again, then continue to cook for about 5 minutes more, or until tender.

Lift the pears into a dish, using a slotted spoon. Bring the remaining liquor to the boil and simmer for about 5 minutes, until syrupy. Pour over the pears, then serve them hot with mascarpone or double cream, or with ice-cream.

Serves 6

Sweet soup of ginger, mango and glass noodles

A deliciously refreshing Asian-inspired dessert that is made in minutes. Instead of bean thread vermicelli (also called cellophane noodles) you could use diced citrus-flavoured jelly (lime, lemon or tangerine).

30 g (1 oz) bean thread vermicelli
6 thin slices fresh ginger
½ cup lime juice
a 415-g (13½ oz) can sliced mango
1 kiwi fruit, peeled and diced

Place the vermicelli in a bowl and cover with boiling water. Leave for a few minutes to soften, then drain. Using a pair of kitchen scissors, chop the vermicelli into manageable lengths.

Combine the ginger, lime juice, two-thirds of the mango and all of its juice, in a food processor with 3–4 ice-cubes. Purée until smooth. Using tongs, divide the noodles evenly between four small bowls. Chop the reserved mango and add this and the kiwi fruit to each dish, then pour on the mango–ginger soup.

Serves 4

Index